Harriet Beecher Stowe

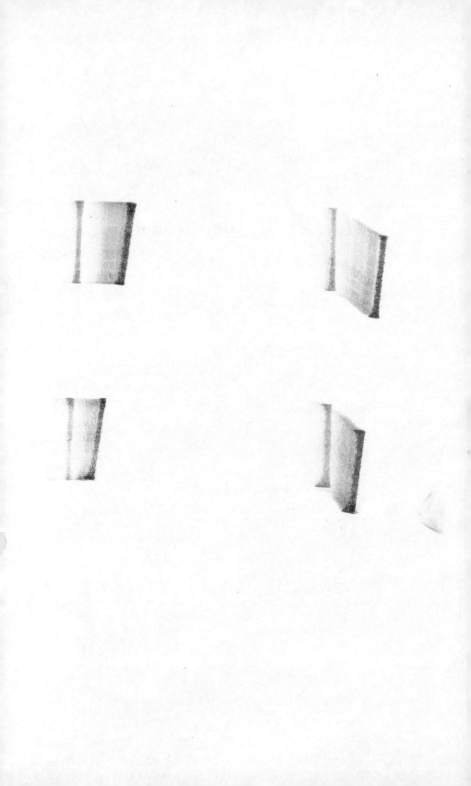

Harriet Beecher Stowe

A Biography by
Noel B. Gerson

PRAEGER PUBLISHERS · NEW YORK

Published in the United States of America in 1976
by Praeger Publishers, Inc.
111 Fourth Avenue, New York, N.Y. 10003

Second printing, 1976

© 1976 by Praeger Publishers, Inc.

Library of Congress Cataloging in Publication Data

Gerson, Noel Bertram, 1914-
    Harriet Beecher Stowe: a biography.

    1. Stowe, Harriet Elizabeth Beecher, 1811-1896—
Biography.
PS2956.G4   818'.3'09 [B]   75-4151
ISBN 0-275-34070-8

Printed in the United States of America

For
Noel Anne

1

"Only now," wrote Henry Adams in 1902, "are we gaining the perspective to discern the trends of the 1800s. But as anyone who has lived during the past fifty years well knows, the Anglo-Saxon world, and much else, have been dominated by the consciences of two unlikely ladies, one English and one American, both born to the purple, both morally determined to recreate civilization in their own image and likeness."

Like Adams's contemporaries, the modern reader easily identifies Queen Victoria as the English lady, but during the better part of a century that has passed since he wrote, recognition of the stature of Victoria's American counterpart has become less widespread. Adams was writing for his own time, however, and his judgment was accurate: Harriet Elizabeth Beecher Stowe left an indelible stamp on her age.

Adams's claim that she was an aristocrat seems at first glance a wild exaggeration. At the beginning of the twentieth century, financial and business tycoons—men like J. Pierpont Morgan, Cornelius Vanderbilt, and members of the Astor clan—were generally regarded as America's bluebloods. But Adams, a direct descendant of two presidents of the United

States, was a Bostonian who admired intellect more than mere wealth, and Harriet Beecher Stowe was a member of a remarkable family that exerted enormous influence over the minds and the souls of several generations of Americans.

Religion was an ever present force in the life of this woman, who was the daughter, sister, wife, and mother of prominent clergymen, and, in this regard, the fact that the men in her family belonged to different Protestant denominations is insignificant. Indeed, her own faith ranged from the Calvinism into which she was born—her father's highly personal religion, rigid yet humanistically permissive—to Episcopalianism, in which she found solace late in life.

What is important is that she was a Beecher, member of a family in which all thirteen children felt a compulsive need to excel. Her father, the Reverend Lyman Beecher, was called "the father of more brains than any other man in America," and the accomplishments of his children still inspire awe.

Hattie, his seventh by Roxanna Foote, the first of his three wives, was the most influential and gained the most enduring renown, even though her next-younger brother, Henry Ward, became perhaps the most prominent clergyman in American history. Catherine, the eldest child, born in 1800, pioneered in the establishment of equal educational opportunities for women. Edward, two years Catherine's junior, was a minister who became a college president, a leader in the antislavery movement, and an editor of note. Charles, four years younger than Hattie, became superintendent of public instruction in Florida and a trailblazer in demanding higher education for blacks. Isabella, born in 1822, was a suffragette who devoted her life to the fight for equal legal rights for women. Born in 1824, Thomas was the youngest of the clan to become famous; a minister, he was among the first to adapt the work of the clergy to the war on urban slums.

A pattern can be seen in these achievements. The Beechers were devoted to the betterment of mankind, to social justice, and to the redress of inequity in the treatment of minority groups. The principles that spurred them on were those of

Lyman Beecher, who was reponsible for the passionate beliefs of his children. His theology was a strange mixture of traditional and personal views, the latter almost unique in his day. The orthodoxies of his Calvinism were stern, and the various congregations he served in his native New England became restive. Beecher moved from one parish to another over a period of many years, and achieved fame as a foe of alcoholic beverages, Roman Catholicism, and what he called "the rationalism of the church movement." In 1832 he and his family went to Cincinnati, where Beecher became president of a new school, the Lane Theological Seminary. His Calvinism proved too weak for Presbyterians of the Middle West. In fact, his liberalism, which extended to a conviction that all men—and women—were equal and deserved equal opportunities, so shocked his colleagues and subordinates that he was brought to trial for heresy, an incident that impelled him to retire at the "early" age of seventy-five.

Harriet Elizabeth, sixth of the then living Beecher children, was born in the parsonage of her father's church at Litchfield, Connecticut, on June 14, 1811. She was named for a sister, born three years earlier, who had died in infancy. Lyman Beecher had already gained renown as an orator, and his sermons were admired for their style, if not for their content—the citizens of Connecticut having become too sophisticated to accept a fire-and-brimstone theology literally. He was a busy man who devoted little time to his children, and Roxanna Beecher was the mainstay of the family.

She gave birth to two more children, Henry Ward and Charles, before she died. Hattie was not yet four and consequently had few specific memories of her mother. Many years later, writing to Charles, she said she recalled an occasion on which Roxanna said, "Remember the Sabbath day; keep it holy, children," an injunction she obeyed literally throughout her own long life.

On another occasion, she and Henry ate some tulip bulbs that a relative had sent to Mrs. Beecher, thinking they were onions but finding their sweet taste disappointing. Roxanna did not punish them but instead described the beautiful flowers that would have grown in the garden the following spring had the children not touched the bulbs. "I remember how drooping and dispirited we all grew at this picture," Hattie wrote.

The younger children were too small to grasp the import of their mother's death but were impressed by the digging of her grave, and a few days later Henry went to work in the garden with a shovel, intending, he said, to dig his way to heaven so he could join Mama. Lyman Beecher was crushed by the tragedy, and the most famous of his children later declared, "I remember hearing him say that after her death his first sensation was a sort of terror, like that of a child suddenly shut out alone in the dark."

Emotionally dependent on his wife, whose strength he had recognized, Lyman Beecher tried to compensate for her loss by paying more attention to the children. But he was uncomfortable in their presence, perhaps because he found it difficult to forget his dignity, and in most of his meetings with them he delivered long monologues that they found it almost impossible to distinguish from sermons. Yet he did manage to communicate his own lofty principles to them and instilled in each a burning desire for recognition based on solid achievement.

The heaviest burden of family responsibility inevitably fell on Catherine, who, at fifteen, was a girl abundantly endowed with determination and energy. She looked after her younger brothers and sisters while continuing her own extensive education, a feat she performed with dexterity. She continued to act as a substitute mother after her father remarried and did not falter when his second wife died and he married for the third time.

Harriet Elizabeth was fond of both her stepmothers and was careful to treat them with deference, but it was Catherine on whom she leaned. This relationship was maintained for many years, and long after Harriet developed her own inner strengths and became independent she continued to lean on sister Catherine.

The younger children had used the attic of the Congregational parsonage as a playroom, but after their mother's death Harriet became so dispirited she rarely went there. Protracted depression was damaging to the soul, Lyman Beecher believed, so the little girl's aunt, Harriet Foote, took her away for a long visit at the home of her grandmother, a farm called Nut Plains, just outside the town of Guilford, Connecticut, on the shore.

Hattie, who had been something of a tomboy, quickly learned to mend her ways. She was forbidden to climb trees in the kitchen yard, fish in Long Island Sound, and romp in the fields with male cousins. Aunt Harriet was a formidable woman, a pillar of the Episcopal church, a firm believer that members of each social class should know their right place and behave accordingly. She was also a loyal citizen of the United States, although she sometimes confused its form of government with that of Great Britain, having been equally devoted to the Crown before the American Revolution.

"According to her views," her niece later recalled, "little girls were to be taught to move very gently, to speak softly and prettily, to say 'yes, ma'am' and 'no, ma'am,' never to tear their clothes, to sew, to knit at regular hours, to go to church on Sunday and make all the responses, and to come home and be catechised."

Harriet Elizabeth had to carry a heavier religious burden than most, for Aunt Harriet compelled her to learn not only the Episcopal catechism but also the Congregational, out of deference to her father. If the child stumbled or erred she would be subjected to the traditional punishment of being sent to bed hungry.

In Grandmother Foote's house, Hattie met black people for the first time—Dinah and Harry, who were a few years her senior and were "bound" or indentured servants. In effect, they were temporary slaves who would have earned their freedom by the time they reached adulthood. They were subjected to Aunt Harriet's catechizing, too, but sat apart from Hattie and were careful to call her "Miss Harriet," it being

Aunt Harriet's unalterable view that servants belonged to a lowly order.

Harriet was pleased with the superior position she enjoyed, but at the same time she suffered her first dilemma. Papa taught that all of God's children were equal, and even Aunt Harriet admitted that Dinah and Harry were children of God. But they were not treated as her equals and were themselves the first to insist they were inferior. Something was amiss, and, in spite of the child's efforts, the problem was too complex for her to solve. She continued to ponder, and years passed before she reached the conclusion that Aunt Harriet's attitudes were wrong.

Grandmother and Aunt Harriet made it their business to teach the four-year-old girl to read, and she was treated to long passages from the King James Bible and the Book of Common Prayer, as well as excerpts from her grandmother's favorites, Dr. Johnson's *Works*, Bishop Heber's *Life*, Buchanan's *Researches in Asia*, and Lowth's *Isaiah*. Of these only the first made any impression on her, and it was her secret conviction that Johnson was dull, a view to which she clung for the rest of her life.

Early in the summer of 1816, Hattie returned to her father's house in Litchfield. She was enrolled in "Ma'am" Kilbourne's school on West Street, to which she walked unaccompanied every day, and was joined there the following year by Henry, whose principal claim to distinction was his refual to wear shoes and stockings on the road.

Not until he reached college would Henry overcome his aversion to learning, but Hattie was an avid student from the outset. Writing about her in November, 1816, Catherine said, "Hattie is a very good girl. She has been to school all this summer, and has learned to read very fluently. She has committed to memory twenty-seven hymns and two long chapters in the Bible. She has a remarkably retentive memory and will make a very good scholar."

Lyman Beecher expected no less of his offspring, but it did not occur to him to open his own library to one so young. By the time Harriet Elizabeth was six she was scouring the house for reading matter, and in the corner of a garret she found a number of barrels filled with old pamphlets and other material her father had used to prepare his sermons. Many were unintelligible to her, including scores of copies of a document entitled, *An appeal on the unlawfulness of a man marrying his wife's sister.*

Ultimately, under a stack of her father's old sermons, she came across a yellowing copy of *The Arabian Nights* and carted it off to her own room with parental approval, her father perhaps believing she was too young to understand it. She was able to follow it completely, however, and read the book many times, on occasion turning to it for solace when her brothers went off on outings and refused to allow her to accompany them.

Before she was eight, she proved to Lyman Beecher's satisfaction that she could master the content of adult books, so he granted her permission to use his library, which contained hundreds of volumes. She lacked the temerity to sit at his desk, where his Bible and concordance lay, and which he used when writing his sermons. Instead, she curled up in a corner of this quiet sanctuary. Most of the essays, sermons, and similar works were too somber for her, but she devoured the folios of grand opera that rested on a lower shelf, and she was overjoyed when her father brought home a two-volume set of short stories, Cotton Mather's *Magnalia.*

She was allowed to remain in the study while Lyman Beecher wrote his sermons, and one day he read the Declaration of Independence to her. Years later she wrote:

> I had never heard of it before, and even now had but a vague idea of what was meant by some parts of it. Still I gathered enough from the recital of abuses and injuries that had driven my nation to this course to feel myself swelling with indignation, and ready with all my little mind and strength to applaud the concluding passage.... I was as ready as any of them to pledge my life, fortune and sacred honor for such a cause. The heroic element was strong in me, having come down by ordinary generation from a long line of Puritan ancestry, and just

> now it made me long to do something, I knew not what:
> to fight for my country, or to make some declaration on
> my own account.

The extent to which that yearning remained prominent in her mind is impossible to determine but can be
exaggerated if common sense is not applied. Countless thousands of children have felt the ambition to perform great
deeds, and it would be absurd to repeat the claim of her early
biographers that Harriet Beecher Stowe pursued her goal
with single-minded ambition. It may not be accidental that
her pen later produced a document that, though far less concise than the Declaration of Independence, was almost
equally influential in shaping the destiny of her country and
the world. But the mantle of future greatness was by no
means visible on her shoulders. By her own account as well as
those of her articulate siblings she was a precocious, slightly
grubby little girl.

Shortly before Harriet Elizabeth's sixth birthday, her
father married again, taking as his wife the pretty Harriet
Porter of Portland, Maine. The new Mrs. Beecher was so
lovely the younger children were in awe of her, and Hattie
later wrote, "She was peculiarly dainty and neat in all her
ways and arrangements, and I used to feel breezy, rough, and
rude in her presence." The lady was also devout and intelligent, and soon won the affection of her bashful
stepchildren.

A new baby, Frederick, joined the family the following
year, but his arrival appears to have been of little concern to
Hattie. Reading was still her favorite pastime, and for diver-
sion she went fishing with her next-oldest brother, George, or
played in the woods with Henry Ward, her most frequent
companion. When Frederick was one year old, he contracted
scarlet fever and died. Hattie suffered from the same disease
but recovered after a long illness, nursed back to good health
by Mrs. Beecher and Catherine.

A letter written by Catherine to a friend that same year,
when Hattie was nine, offers a revealing glimpse of the girl's

developing personality: "Last week we interred Tom cat junior with funeral honors by the side of old Tom of happy memory. Our Harriet is chief mourner always at their funerals." The Beechers, like children of comparable station in England, were taught reserve and believed it improper to show their emotions. But ordinary rules did not apply to Hattie, already winning recognition as the brightest of the brilliant, and she openly gave vent to her feelings whenever she wished.

Much as she enjoyed going on hikes with her brothers, when she reached the age of ten Hattie no longer had time for such adventures. She was enrolled now in John Brace's Litchfield Academy, where she stood first in academic achievement. She continued to read constantly, too, and was allowed to sit at her father's feet when he debated theological questions with fellow clergymen, a pastime she enjoyed. Her brothers, without exception, were destined to become clergymen, but Catherine observed that Hattie, at ten, was a more accomplished theologian than any of them.

In 1822, when Harriet Elizabeth was eleven, Mrs. Beecher gave birth to a daughter, Isabella. Hattie lost her often considered privileged position as the family's youngest girl and was secretly relieved. She hated being babied, and had long wanted to be accepted as her brothers' equal. Now, overnight, she achieved that status. She was also required to take care of the baby for several hours after school each day, which helped her mature more rapidly, according to her own account. Amazingly, she was able to take care of her chores without losing any precious reading time.

Before Harriet was eleven, she wrote her first composition, responding with astonishing agility to the ordeal of ordering her thoughts on paper. The disciplines of writing seemed to come naturally to her. Even at that age she could spend long hours with a pen in her hand and then return to her labors after a short respite to revise what she had already put on paper.

Harriet achieved her first triumph as an author at the age of twelve. All students at the Litchfield Academy were required to submit essays at the end of the term, and two papers were read at the graduation exercises by the headmaster, John Brace. The first prize was awarded by the unanimous vote of the judges to the author of a document entitled "Can the Immortality of the Soul Be Proved by the Light of Nature?" This essay of twenty-five hundred words was cogent and cohesive, and the audience applauded when Brace finished his reading.

Then Harriet Elizabeth Beecher was revealed as the author, and the delighted smile of her proud father was a reward she cherished as long as she lived. Neither the honors nor the successes she won in later life meant as much to her, and, in effect, her career was determined.

The most courageous of Lyman Beecher's children, in the opinion of her brothers and sisters, was Catherine, the eldest. Having suffered a tragedy early in life, when the man to whom she was engaged died in a shipwreck, she never married, and instead devoted more than a half-century to helping others. Catherine had one of the family's better minds, which meant that few people were her intellectual peers, and she was endowed with the crusading spirit of the Beechers as well as the determination to allow nothing to stand between her and her goals.

This formidable lady was self-educated, in the main, and she knew from her own experience that educational opportunities for women were virtually nonexistent in the United States. Members of her sex were expected to cultivate domestic virtues and social graces to prepare themselves for lives as wives, mothers, and housekeepers. Catherine was not opposed to marriage, but she believed with a Beecher's passion that women had the right to develop and use their minds. Far ahead of her time, she was convinced that women of talent and ambition should be encouraged to pursue careers of their own;

indeed, she advocated the revolutionary theory that career and marriage did not exclude each other.

It was not enough for a Beecher to form an opinion. Each felt compelled to act in accordance with his view and convert others to it. Catherine set an example for her younger brothers and sisters by renting a large room in Hartford, Connecticut's capital and largest city, a metropolitan center with a population of more than twenty-five thousand. Located on Main Street, above Sheldon and Colton's harness store, the building was almost directly opposite Christ Church. There, in the late summer of 1824, she established a school for teenaged girls.

One of her original pupils was her thirteen-year-old sister, Harriet Elizabeth, who paid no tuition fee. The family's funds were limited, but Lyman Beecher was ingenious. He worked out an arrangement with Isaac D. Bull, a Hartford wholesale druggist, whereby Hattie would live with the Bull family, whose daughter would take up residence with the Beechers in Litchfield and attend a seminary for young ladies there.

The Bulls were devout Congregationalists, much interested in music, and their home was so neat, Harriet later observed, that her stepmother would have enjoyed living there. The girl was given her own bedroom, which delighted her, and soon developed rapport with the entire family.

Two schoolmates became Hattie's intimates, and they are worthy of mention because her friendship with them lasted for the rest of their lives. One was Catherine Ledyard Cogswell, the daughter of a distinguished physician and a member of one of Connecticut's oldest families. The other was Georgiana May, whose father had died. Both girls had strong, independent minds, and refused to be cowed by a precocious Beecher, which made Hattie appreciate them all the more.

Philosophy and languages, among them Latin, French, and Italian, formed the core of the curriculum at Catherine Beecher's school. Harriet Elizabeth discovered poetry, particularly that of Lord Byron, and not only read all she could find but dreamed of becoming a poet herself. She began working on an epic poem she called *Cleon,* the story of a Greek nobleman at the court of the Roman Emperor Nero, who became a convert to Christianity after prolonged soul-searching.

This work has been lost to posterity because Hattie made the mistake of writing some of her verses at school. Catherine pounced on the notebook one day, read the contents, and confiscated it. Poetry was rubbish, she declared, and pupils should rather spend their time studying such useful subjects as logic. Harriet Elizabeth obviously had too little to occupy her active mind, so she was directed not only to master the abstractions of Butler's *Analogy* but to teach a course on the book to girls of her own age. Harriet Elizabeth accomplished the terrifying assignment by keeping one chapter ahead of her students.

She, too, was a stubborn Beecher, however, and refused to abandon poetry. She was careful to read and write it behind the closed door of her bedroom, but at no time did she fall behind in her school work. Harriet was expected to sleep eight hours each night but soon found she needed only six. She discovered, too, that it was easier to concentrate on her own writing late at night, when the house was quiet, and she began to form the habits to which she would adhere throughout the better part of her professional life.

"It was at about this time that I first believed myself to be a Christian," she later wrote. Returning to Litchfield for a summer vacation, she attended church services, as she had done since early childhood. All members of the family old enough to walk sat quietly in their pew every Sunday, and any child who fidgeted during Papa's sermon was sent to bed without Sunday dinner.

"Most of my father's sermons were as unintelligible for me as if he had spoken in Choctaw," Harriet admitted. They were intended for the edification of adults, but it was expected that the youngsters remain motionless. Occasionally, however, Dr. Beecher preached what he called a "frame sermon," one that grew out of his deep feelings of the moment and could neither be prepared in advance nor later repeated.

On this occasion, the girl declared, she was "drawn to listen by a certain pathetic earnestness in his voice." Hair-splitting distinctions and dialectic subtleties were forgotten. At his best, Lyman Beecher was a powerful orator whose simplicity and tenderness could move an entire congregation to weep. Harriet wept harder than the rest, and when she returned home she told her father she had become a wholehearted convert.

He alone accepted her staement at face value. His friend the pastor of the First Congregational Church in Hartford was openly suspicious, and so was sister Catherine. As Hattie remarked many years later, sheep didn't come into the fold of their own volition, but had to be chased all over the lot by the shepherd.

In the early months of 1826, the girl added mathematics to her studies, even though she loathed the subject. In June she would be fifteen, and her superior scholarship assured her of a future place on Catherine's faculty. No other career was open to Harriet and other similarly talented young women.

Late in February, 1826, Dr. Beecher stunned his family by accepting a call to the Hanover Street Church in Boston, where he would have free use of a small parsonage and receive a generous salary of $2,000 per year, and a "settlement" of $500, a cash payment that would enable him to make the move without out-of-pocket expense. He had concluded that he could no longer afford to live in Litchfield on the tiny salary he received there. Harriet was much upset, as were her brothers and sisters. The Litchfield parsonage was the only home they had ever known, and, much as they sympathized with Papa's financial plight and applauded his decision to better himself, they felt the family was breaking up.

Catherine's affairs prospered, and by February, 1827, she was actively constructing her own school building. The Hartford Female Seminary, as the institution was called, had as many teachers and students as it could accommodate, and an Englishwoman who lived and taught in New York would come to Hartford within a few months, bringing her pupils with her.

Harriet had been withdrawn from Catherine's school, however, in order to go to Boston to live with her father and stepmother and attend a day school there. She was in a state of emotional upset common among girls in their mid-teens, and her melancholy is best illustrated by an excerpt from a long letter she wrote to Catherine: "I don't know as I am fit for anything, and I have thought that I could wish to die young, and let the remembrance of me and my faults perish in the grave, rather than live, as I fear I do, a trouble to every one. You don't know how perfectly wretched I often feel: so useless, so weak, so destitute of all energy. Mama often tells me that I am a strange, inconsistent being."

Catherine was a brisk woman who tolerated no nonsense. She realized that their stepmother, who had small children of her own and faced problems of her own in adjusting to a new congregation, had little time to spend with a moody teenager. Catherine was surrounded by adolescents, and in a letter to her brother Edward from her school in Hartford she outlined Harriet's needs.

> If she could come here it might be the best thing for her, for she can talk freely to me. I can get her books, and Catherine Cogswell, Georgiana May, and her friends here could do more for her than any one in Boston, for they love her, and she loves them very much. Georgiana's difficulties are different from Harriet's: she is speculating about doctrines, etc. Harriet will have young society here all the time, which she cannot have at home, and I think cheerful and amusing friends will do much for her. I can do better in preparing her to teach ... than anyone else, for I best know what is needed.

For a time Hattie refused to leave Boston, failing to understand that a possible cause of her depression had been the family's move from Litchfield, which had destroyed her sense of security. She continued to cling to her father, and she was welcome to stay in Boston as long as she wished, even though the parsonage there was cramped.

In the spring of 1827, however, she was persuaded to visit Grandmother Foote at her farm near Guilford. Georgiana May accompanied her, and after a holiday of several weeks her spirits began to improve. By summer she was growing restless, and in the autumn of 1827 she finally returned to Hartford.

The construction of the new Hartford Female Seminary had been completed, the school was in full operation, and Catherine Beecher, together with the three ladies who served as her faculty, lived in a small house behind the main building. Harriet moved in with them, assuming a work load that must have taxed the energies of even a Beecher. She resumed her own studies, taking courses in Latin, French, mathematics, and Italian. She earned her keep by acting as an assistant to the teachers and by tutoring pupils on the side. Moreover, having discovered she had a natural talent as an artist, she made preparations, under Catherine's tutelage, to teach painting and drawing. In her less than plentiful spare time she tried her hand at still-life painting in both oil and watercolors.

During this same year, her faith in God was fervently renewed, and she found the time to write long letters about religion to her brothers Edward and Henry Ward. In one communication, she thanked Edward for revealing to her that he had found literature a snare. She, too, had discovered that reading for pleasure took precious hours that could be spent in Bible study, and she promised to give up the pernicious habit. It was a pledge she could not keep, however.

In 1828, soon after her seventeenth birthday, Harriet visited George, who was earning a living as an instructor at the boy's academy in Groton, Massachusetts, so that he could resume his own higher education. She also spent several days in Boston, where she saw her new infant brother, James; she subsequently wrote to Georgiana May, "He has nothing to distinguish him from forty other babies, except a very large pair of blue eyes and an uncommonly fair complexion, which is of no sort of use or advantage to a man or boy."

While paying a second visit to George, she was offered the post of headmistress of the small academy for females being established there. She seriously contemplated making the move, although she had no friends in Groton, but was soon discouraged from doing so by Catherine and Dr. Beecher, who pointed out that a strange community was no place for a girl of her age, that she was lacking in the qualifications necessary for the position, and that George was not sufficiently mature to act as her chaperon.

Harriet returned to Hartford without further ado and resumed her life at the Female Seminary. This year she roomed with three teachers, one of them a girl only two years her senior. The enrollment increased again, the faculty became larger, and Harriet had to assume greater responsibilities, adding a class in rhetoric to her already full schedule of teaching. She spent her evenings preparing for her next teaching assignment and studying for the courses she was taking in French and Italian. She had few opportunities to paint, but in her correspondence with Grandmother Foote, her father, and her brothers she still found time to speculate at length on the nature of God's love for man.

Still introspective, Harriet was developing an ability to see her own faults. She brooded more than was good for her peace of mind, she wrote, and she knew she was too sensitive to the opinions of others. As long as she did what she knew was right, she declared, she shouldn't care what others thought of her actions.

By 1829 Harriet's routines were established and for the next few years, until 1832, they changed only slightly. By the time she was twenty-one, she had given up all of her own studies except French and had become a full-time teacher. Sufficiently acute as an art critic to realize she lacked the talent to pursue an active career as a painter, she continued to teach drawing and painting, along with other subjects. No member of Catherine's busy faculty could afford to be too much of a specialist.

The long summer vacations were spent at the parsonage in Boston and visiting brothers who had churches of their own in various parts of New England. The shorter winter and spring vacations Harriet spent with Grandmother Foote in Guilford.

Harriet had abandoned her attempt to give up literature, and, resuming the habits of childhood, read everything and anything she could find in both English and French. Dr. Johnson was more palatable to her now and she enjoyed the poetry of Alexander Pope, but Dean Swift was too savage for her taste, as was Voltaire, and the harsh, bawdy realities of Henry Fielding disturbed her. She appreciated the works of Shakespeare, overlooking vulgarities that offended nineteenth-century sensibilities because he was regarded as the greatest of authors. In the main, it was the classics that soothed her, and she felt most at home with Ovid and Homer.

At twenty-one Harriet—only the family called her Hattie—was a handsome young woman of medium height, with a slender, graceful figure. Her forehead was high, her nose straight and clean-cut, her mouth gentle but firm; high cheekbones gave her face an oval shape. Contemporary styles did much, however, to detract from her femininity: Clothes were full, and they hid her figure, her hair was parted in the middle and drooped unbecomingly in ringlets at the sides. At no time did she wear cosmetics of any kind. It is unlikely that she regarded herself as attractive, since proper young New England ladies did not dwell on such matters. If she thought of men and marriage she admitted it in none of her correspondence, and it must be assumed she was true to her training and banished any such notions that may have crept into her mind.

Harriet was an indefatigable letter-writer, corresponding at astonishing length with her father and grandmother, her brothers and sisters, new and old friends. It cannot yet have crossed her mind that she was a compulsive writer with the talent and inclinations of a professional author. At twenty-one she was just beginning to realize that an inner compulsion forced her to reply within a day or two to any letter she received.

Her correspondence was somewhat more erudite and a trifle more sophisticated than it had been a few years earlier, thanks to her reading, and she occasionally referred to such subjects as Italian architecture, French natural philosophy, and English jurisprudence. She demonstrated no awareness of domestic and foreign politics, economics, or issues of the day, and if she knew of it at all, contemporary American and English literature lay outside her sphere of interest.

Her letters, many of them two or three thousand words long, are concentrated on two subjects, religion and her own emotions, and frequently they are intertwined. At what to most modern readers seems interminable length run Harriet's repetitive discussions of God's love for man, her adoration of Christ, and her attempts to "purify and reform" her "sinfulness, waywardness and folly" so that she would more closely resemble him. Indeed, correspondence was Harriet's only outlet for the many emotions seething within her, and her letters almost literally throb with intensity of feeling. She professed to be content with her life as a teacher, and there is no hint that, unlike Catherine, she did not wish to remain a spinster for the rest of her days. The Beecher discipline, the reserve that New Englanders regarded as natural had had their effect, and whenever Harriet became restless she could only blame her "sinfulness, waywardness and folly."

At this time, as she wrote years later to Charles, she at last began to understand her father. She saw a man continually at war with alcohol, with the "godless" faculty of Harvard College (who were scarcely aware of his existence), with Unitarians on the left and Roman Catholics on the right, with anyone who broke the Sabbath, with politicians because they took the name of the Lord in vain, and with fellow Calvinists for being too conservative or too radical. She realized for the first time that he, too, sometimes suffered from melancholy, which he overcame by pitching gravel from one side of the cellar to the other or sawing wood for hours at a time. She saw a shabby, intense man, his pockets filled with scribbled notes he could not read, a man so busy battling the world that he had to improvise many of his sermons.

Above all, she saw a man so busy fighting his concept of the devil in various guises that he was scarcely aware of her existence. She not only saw but understood and forgave him for his absentmindedness, and a long-felt secret hurt was dissipated. Harriet freed herself in the process, and this new maturity enabled her to face the greatest challenge she had known since the death of her mother.

In the summer of 1832, members of the board of trustees of a new, as yet unopened school, the Lane Theological Seminary, located in Cincinnati, Ohio, made Lyman Beecher a dazzling offer. They wanted him to become president of the institution, whose buildings were already completed, and they promised to raise the enormous sum of $70,000 for faculty salaries and other expenses.

Dr. Beecher was excited and flattered, but withheld his decision until he visited Cincinnati, met other trustees, and inspected the property. He was accompanied by Catherine, who saw an opportunity to fulfill her own dream—that of establishing a full-fledged college for women under the auspices of the seminary.

During their absence, Harriet reviewed her own life and found little that satisfied her. She openly envied her sister Mary, who had married a successful young Hartford attorney, Thomas Perkins, and was living a normal, happy life. There was little normality in Harriet's own existence. The quarters she shared with the other faculty members at Catherine's Female Seminary were crowded, and these women had little patience with her moods, sometimes calling her hysterical. She suspected they were right and wondered if Catherine Cogswell failed to answer her letters because she had been overwhelmed and repelled by page after page of emotional outbursts.

She had never been close to her brother William, and Edward, who had just been made minister of the Park Street Church in Boston, constantly preached theology to her. Henry Ward and Charles, her favorites, were attending college at Amherst.

Harriet had achieved an understanding of her father but as yet failed to understand herself. Apparently it never crossed her mind that she was leading a stultifying existence at the seminary, where she worked from early morning until late at night, often snatching meals in the classroom. Only recently had Catherine Beecher realized that something was amiss and had made arrangements with a nearby stable to provide horses for faculty members who wanted physical exercise.

But Harriet had been "too tired" to ride, and was "too tired" now to do more than scribble very long letters to her grandmother, her brothers, and Georgiana. Neither then nor at any other time in her life did she realize she was using chronic fatigue to shield her from the world beyond her circumscribed sphere. By the time she became the most famous American woman of her era, it was too late: She suffered frequently from fatigue, and nothing relieved its symptoms. Harriet was frail, the family said, accepting her condition as a fact of life. For many years, Harriet herself made no attempt to seek alleviation of the ailment, neither trying the various elixirs popular at the time nor seeking the aid of a physician.

Obviously Harriet was a victim of the Beecher curse—burning ambition. Like her father and her siblings, she sought renown. The acquisition of wealth did not particularly appeal to her, any more than it did to her brothers and sisters. Reared in genteel poverty and taught from earliest childhood to make their peace with God, they showed little interest in material possessions. Even in later years, when Harriet enjoyed a huge income, she cared little about money or what it could buy. It was fame alone that mattered, and for eight years, from the age of thirteen to the age of twenty-one, she had worked incessantly, preparing herself for an uncertain future. Unhappily, she had found no specific goal, no realm in which to excel. She had the good sense to realize that her paintings of bowls of fruit, though pretty, were ordinary. She had been trained as a teacher, and in that profession she was overshadowed by the aggressive Catherine, who intimidated her.

Only in her correspondence had she found a partial outlet for her seething emotions. Lifelong spinsterhood seemed inevitable. No man had ever shown the slightest interest in her, for her life at a girl's school made it difficult for her to meet anyone of the opposite sex.

Harriet might have suffered another breakdown had the dramatic change in the family's situation not taken her mind off her own problems. Dr. Beecher and Catherine returned to Boston filled with enthusiasm for the new venture. The Lane Theological Seminary plant was even more attractive than they imagined. The wooded campus was beautiful. The buildings were large, and the house in which the family would reside was comfortable. Ample space was available for the women's school Catherine wanted to found; for this, she was already making plans, intending to hire faculty members who would confine their teaching to single subjects, which was the practice at Harvard, Yale, and other colleges on the Eastern Seaboard.

Dr. Beecher and Catherine portrayed Cincinnati as a virtual paradise. The bustling Ohio River city, gateway to the South and to the West, was the Athens of the West, if not the Athens of all America. Approximately twice the size of Hartford, with a population of fifty thousand and growing rapidly, it was a major railroad center as well as a river port, a manufacturing center of consequence, and a natural point of conjunction for the disparate cultures of North and South.

No longer a frontier town, Cincinnati was on the way to acquiring a high patina of culture. The Beechers had no interest in the theater, sharing the view of many New Englanders that the stage was depraved, but both Catherine and Harriet approved of the many musicales and lectures given there. The intellectual life of the city was not as stimulating as that of Boston and Cambridge, but the family had not participated extensively in the activities open to them there.

Best of all, Papa and Catherine said, Cincinnati was a beehive of Christianity. There was a large core of devout, some calling themselves Congregationalists, others preferring to be known as Presbyterians, but all shared Dr. Beecher's strict Calvinistic beliefs. Dr. Beecher, infinitely more narrow-minded than most of his sons and daughters, who rebelled against their father's violent prejudices, was also pleased to reveal that, although there were communities of the heathen in Cincinnati—among them Papists, near-Papist Episcopalians, Unitarians, Jews, and a scattering of other radicals—they were of no consequence. True Christians were everywhere and held up the pillars of the new Athens with firm hands.

So the family would move. Accompanying Dr. and Mrs. Beecher would be their two young children Isabella and James. Esther Beecher, the clergyman's spinster sister, would make her home with them. George, his undergraduate degree in hand, would follow the family vocation and enroll in the seminary as a candidate for a divinity degree. Catherine would be a member of the party, and would found her college for women. She was to be accompanied by Harriet Elizabeth Beecher, who would serve as her first assistant, acting as a college administrator and teaching courses in a subject to be determined when other members of the faculty were hired.

"The moral destiny of our nation and all our institutions and hopes and the world's hopes turns on the character of the West, and the competition now is for that of preoccupancy in the education of the rising generation, in which Catholics and infidels have got the start of us," Lyman Beecher declared. Exhorting William and Edward to follow him to the

Harriet Beecher Stowe

Promised Land, he announced his intention of finding pulpits for them so that they might join him in waging the good fight. His own enthusiasm was so great he failed to notice their reluctance to leave the East. Apparently it slipped his mind, too, that until the presidency of Lane had been offered to him he had deplored the westward migration because it had depleted the ranks of the faithful in New England. Consistency never having been one of his virtues, Dr. Beecher was untroubled by his abrupt reversal.

The family, nine in all, left Boston in early October, 1832, and spent a month on the road before they reached their destination. Their journey was leisurely, and they paused from time to time to spend a few days with good Congregational and Presbyterian friends. Their first stop was New York, too large and bustling for Harriet, who complained that its superabundance of energy exhausted her. Philadelphia was gentler, its pace similar to that of Hartford and Boston, and she felt at home there.

She made no comments on the towns of Harrisburg or Wheeling, writing only about the friends she visited there. The first mountains she had ever seen, the Alleghenies failed to impress her, and she made no mention in her correspondence of the mighty Ohio, even though the last stage of the journey was made on the river by paddle-wheeler. In spite of the many childhood hours she had spent in the woods, the maturing Harriet was far more interested in people than in places. Occasionally, she rhapsodized briefly over a flower that caught her eye, but she devoted long paragraphs to wry descriptions of ladies, gentlemen, and small children like James, whose direct, rather abrupt manners she found preferable to the often ambivalent social behavior and attitudes of adults.

A two-story brick house in Walnut Hills, a short distance from the Lane campus, awaited the Beechers, and four servants had already been hired for them, two youths of German descent, an Irish immigrant girl, and a girl, even more recently arrived, from Wales.

More than a score of relatives who lived in Cincinnati were on hand to greet the new arrivals, as were the Lane trustees and the vestrymen of the Second Presbyterian Church. Representatives of the rival First Church were conspicuous in their absence.

Two of the more prominent Cincinnati members of the family were brothers of the first Mrs. Beecher, John and Samuel Foote. Uncle Samuel was the most fascinating person Harriet and her brothers and sisters had ever met. During his few visits to Litchfield, before he had settled in the West, they had been awed by him as well as by his exotic gifts, which included slippers from Morocco and a silver ingot on a chain, which he had found in Turkey.

Dr. Beecher did not entirely approve of Samuel, even though he had earned a fortune in Cincinnati, attended church regularly, and was a Lane trustee as well as a Second Presbyterian vestryman. He had not only traveled extensively in Europe, the Near East, and Africa, but he saw virtues in people everywhere. He numbered Roman Catholics and Jews in Cincinnati among his close friends and unfailingly counterattacked when the prejudiced—among them Dr. Beecher—made their feelings known. He dared to admit that some infidel Muslims in Constantinople were dear friends, too, and it was said that he and a Turkish girl had engaged in a spirited romance.

Samuel Foote loved the theater and made a point of repeatedly inviting Catherine and Harriet to attend performances of Shakespeare's plays with him. Catherine refused, but Harriet eventually weakened and was enchanted by *Hamlet* and *Romeo and Juliet*. She was unable to agree with Papa and Catherine that the theater was wicked and sinful, but she wisely kept her opinions to herself.

Thanks to Uncle Samuel, too, she read the novels of Sir Walter Scott and the poetry of Lord Byron, and because of his persistence she became a member of one of his favorite organizations, the Semi-Colon Club, where discussions of literature were held each week. Catherine attended one or two sessions, too, but she was bored by them and did not return.

Because Sarah Worthington King, Mrs. Beecher's cousin, was one of the officers of the club, Dr. Beecher was reluctant to ask Harriet to keep her distance from the organization.

Unlike most such clubs, the Semi-Colon was made up of people actively interested in contemporary literature, including a number of professional authors and editors. One of the leading members was Caroline Lee Hentz, who wrote short stories regularly for the *Western Monthly Magazine*. She was also a successful dramatist, and one of her plays, *De Lara; or, the Moorish Bride,* won a prize of $500; later, it was produced successfully in Philadelphia and Boston, although it failed in New York. Another member, Judge James Hall, editor of the *Western Monthly,* not only encouraged Harriet to write professionally but bought and published her first story.

From a young lawyer who belonged to the club, Salmon P. Chase—not yet twenty-five but already a leader in the anti-slavery movement—a wide-eyed Harriet first learned about the abuses of the slave-holding system that made the economy of the South profitable. Soon to become active in the abolitionist movement, Chase, who would later become United States senator, Secretary of the Treasury, and, ultimately, Chief Justice of the Supreme Court, remained on friendly terms with Harriet throughout their long lives.

Harriet emerged sufficiently from her shell to feel at ease with most of the club's regular members, but she developed a strong dislike for Mrs. Hentz, who held pronounced pro-slavery views. After moving a few years later to the Deep South, she wrote a series of novels which emphasized the social benefits of the slave system to blacks as well as whites. Harriet soon felt a quiet contempt for her.

She responded with great warmth, however, to a married couple who were fellow newcomers to the Semi-Colon Club. Calvin Ellis Stowe was professor of Biblical literature at Lane, a tall man with a commanding presence, a leonine head, a full beard, and a deep, resonant voice. He was a forceful speaker, and in consequence tended to dominate any social

gathering he attended. Only those who knew him best realized that in actuality he was a reserved, shy man who tended
to shun the real world by taking refuge in flights of idealistic
fancy.

His wife, the former Eliza Tyler, was a member of one of
the most prominent families in the Presbyterian movement in
the United States. She was fragile and tiny, and her contemporaries described her as lovely, perhaps because of her
ethereal, elflike nature. She and Harriet had somewhat
similar personalities, which both were quick to recognize,
and within a surprisingly short time they became close
friends. Harriet was in awe of Dr. Stowe, and her relations
with him appear to have been formal.

In spite of the social distractions, greater by far than any
she had ever-known, Harriet's work came first, and there
was enough of it to inundate her. Catherine had intended to
act only in a supervisory capacity in the establishment of the
school she called the Western Female Institute, but she was
incapable of delegating authority. She plunged into the labor
of hiring faculty, recruiting students, and making living
arrangements for both groups. Harriet took care of countless
details, acting as an extension of Catherine, and dutifully
informed her sister of every move she made.

Among the many problems the institute faced was a lack
of textbooks regarded as suitable for serious-minded young
ladies. Harriet accepted the assignment of relieving at least a
part of this deficiency by writing a geography book that
would put the world in perspective for students whose frames
of reference tended to be hazy.

Here, Dr. Beecher saw an opportunity to proselytize for
the Presbyterian cause. Harriet privately disagreed with
him, believing she should present students with a portrait of
the world as it was. She would not have dared to argue with
Papa, but she began to develop her own way of achieving
what she wanted. Her smile bland, she kept her own counsel
and wrote what she felt was appropriate.

The geography, published at Lane's expense, was a dry,
academic study devoid of all personality, and it produced no

income for its author, although it was used by institute students as a text for many years. It is important only as a curiosity and is significant for no reason other than that it was Harriet Elizabeth Beecher's first book.

Harried and overworked again, her social life circumscribed and her day-to-day existence dominated by Papa and Catherine, Harriet again suffered from fatigue. In his biography of her, published during her lifetime, in 1889, Harriet's son the Reverend Charles Edward Stowe said that "her ill health was largely due to unregulated and unrestrained feeling. She lived overmuch in her emotions."

His analysis was accurate enough, but shallow. Harriet knew herself far better, as she indicated in a frank letter to her dear friend Georgiana. Her insight sharpened by extensive reading from the works of the emotional, sharp-witted French novelist and essayist Mme. de Staël, she indicated that her depression was caused by the self-confinement created by "the constant habits of self-government which the rigid forms of our society demand. They are repressed and they burn inward till they burn the very soul.... All that is impassioned in admiration of nature, of writing, of character, in devotional thought and emotion, or in the emotions of affections, I have felt... till my mind is exhausted, and seems to be sinking into deadness. Half of my time I am glad to remain in a listless vacancy, to busy myself with trifles, since thought is pain, and emotion is pain."

Yet it is easy to exaggerate the significance of this declaration, which was quoted by virtually all of the earlier biographers. Certainly Harriet was sincere, but it is possible both that she was more of a victim of her era than she realized and that her inner plight was less grim than she pictured it. Twenty-three when she wrote the letter, she had never been courted by a man, and in spite of her new friendships was still living in emotional isolation. On the other hand, young women of the period poured out their hearts to their dearest friends in a similar vein, and thus Harriet was reflecting the conventions of the times.

This is not to say that her depression and consequent fatigue were other than genuine. But her existence was so busy that she had few hours in the day to remain in a "listless vacancy." She was one of the busiest of busy Beechers, arising at six in the morning, reaching her office at seven, and frequently remaining there until late at night. Catherine had realized that such a restricted and intense existence was bad for one's health, but Harriet's habits had by now become compulsive, and not even her sister could budge her until she completed her day's quota of work.

She was inclined toward melancholy, to be sure, but even a robust person in the best of emotional health might well feel weary and depressed after following her exacting regimen for week after unrelieved week. The few hours spent at the Semi-Colon Club meetings could not compensate for a life of unrelieved drabness.

Within limits, Harriet tried to improve her spirits. The fashions of the 1830s were hideously unattractive, and a proper young lady dared not venture beyond the strict limits of acceptability. All the same, Harriet tried to express a measure of individuality in her dress: most of her costumes, long-sleeved and plain, with high necks and full skirts, were suitable attire for the spinster daughter of the president of a Calvinist theological seminary. Nevertheless, she showed a spark of imagination in putting together a wardrobe of exclusively white dresses, over which she wore a small apron of black silk.

She was more attractive than she realized, and life in the West was freer, less repressive than in New England. The seething ferment she had been undergoing for several years was demanding an outlet. Harriet was on the brink of finding it—and herself.

In the July, 1833, edition of the *Western Monthly Magazine* there appeared a short article, written in a satirical vein, and vaguely reminiscent in style of the eighteenth-century prose works of Addison and Steele. Its subject was the misuse of punctuation and the atrocious grammar in contemporary American literature. The piece was labored, and, in spite of an attempt to strike an informal note, it was rigid.

The article contained a dedication, "To Catherine," but was unsigned. Judge Hall would have been delighted to give her public credit for her piece, but Harriet was not yet ready to permit her name to be seen in public. It was enough to know that people were reading her work, and she was elated when she received the staggering sum of $50 for the article. She had written it in only a few hours, and her salary for an entire year of hard labor at the institute was a mere $500.

Judge Hall's payment made Harriet a professional author, and thereafter she regarded herself strictly in that light, never considering writing a mere avocation, much less an escape from teaching. Writing was her craft, the thoughts she expressed on paper were of interest to general readers, and for this reason she deserved hard cash in return. From the outset of her unique career she suffered no shyness on that score.

Fiction, including both the novel and the short story, stood high on Lyman Beecher's endless list of prejudices. It ranked after the theater as iniquitous and depraved but nevertheless was to be shunned by Christians endeavoring to lead moral lives. This attitude, a refrain in countless sermons, makes it surprising that the magical words *"by Harriet Elizabeth Beecher"* eventually appeared on a short story published in the *Western Monthly* in November, 1833. What Dr. Beecher thought of Harriet's apostasy was never revealed in her correspondence or elsewhere, but it can be imagined. Her silence on the matter may have been well and wisely based on the belief that delicacy is the better part of valor.

Called "A New England Tale" when it first appeared, the piece was retitled "Uncle Tim" in the first edition of her collected short stories, *The Mayflower,* published in 1843; Harriet changed it again—this time to "Uncle Lot"—when the second edition came out in 1855. Judge Hall appears to have been a one-price editor, and again gave her fifty dollars for submitting it for publication in his magazine.

When Hall encouraged her to write the story, she faced a dilemma. Should she write of foreign places, as Washington Irving had done? No, Irving had lived in Europe and knew the locales; besides, he had earned his initial reputation writing about the America he knew. Wrestling with the problem, Harriet pondered on paper in a letter to the faithful Georgiana.

> And so I am to write a story—but of what, and where? Shall it be radiant with the sky of Italy? or eloquent with the *beau idéal* of Greece? Shall it breathe odor and languor from the orient, or chivalry from the occident? or gayety from France? or vigor from England?
>
> No, no; these are all too old, too romance-like, too obviously picturesque for me. No; let me turn to my own land—my own New England; the land of bright fires and

strong hearts; the land of *deeds* and not of words; the
land of fruits and not of flowers; the land often spoken
against, yet always respected. . . .

Now, from this heroic apostrophe, you may suppose
that I have something heroic to tell. By no means. It is
merely a little introductory breeze of patriotism, such as
occasionally brushes over every mind, bearing on its
wings the remembrance of all we ever loved or cherished in the land of our early years; and if it should seem
to be rodomontade to any people in other parts of the
earth, let them only imagine it to be said about "Old
Kentucky," old England, or any other corner of the world
in which they happened to be born, and they will find it
quite rational.

The 22-year-old girl showed sound common sense
in turning away from such subjects as the Byron-inspired
Cleon of her adolescence and instead concentrating on the
kinds of people and backgrounds she actually knew.

It is important to remember that throughout her career,
from this first short story to later works of both fiction and
nonfiction that sold millions of copies, Harriet Elizabeth
Beecher was not striving for artistic effects. In her fiction she
had a story to tell; in her nonfiction she had direct points to
make. At no time was her technique polished. Her dialogue
was careless and her punctuation abominable. It was she who
made the dash fashionable, using it with abandon, and in this
she was copied by hundreds of writers, thereby adding to the
miseries suffered by their editors.

In spite of her many shortcomings as a writer—her often
larger-than-life characters, her cliché-ridden plots, her ornate style—the strength of her work, and ultimately her popularity, derived from her ability to present characters, situa-
tions, and backgrounds that impressed her readers as authentic.
This core of realism made it possible, thematically, for her to
express her religion-inspired idealism, concealing it sufficiently to make it palatable, at least to readers of her own time.

The modern reader too often forgets that her nine-teenth-century audience was composed of men and women who instantly recognized her characters as people whom they knew or knew of. Her descriptions of places were sometimes sketchy and even sloppily delineated, but she had a genius for grasping the essence of a place, for mentioning details so familiar to readers that they found it easy to imagine them-selves there.

No discussion of the impact of her fiction would be complete without mentioning that it was she, more than any other American author, whose work broke down the prej-udices of the early nineteenth century against the novel and the short story. This did not happen, it is true, until the tidal-wave popularity of *Uncle Tom's Cabin* swept away the barriers that had confined fiction for the better part of a half-century. But qualities that contributed to the unprec-edented, never repeated success of her biggest-selling, most influential work were present in her earliest fiction, too.

Certainly the flavor of New England is apparent in the following exchange between Uncle Tim and his daughter, Grace, a heroine similar to the author herself; her romance with a hero not unlike the man Harriet knew best, Lyman Beecher, forms the core of the story.

Having come home, Uncle Tim sees an array of pies and rows of cakes on the kitchen table.

> "Grace—Grace—Grace, I say! What is all this here flum-mery for?"
>
> "Why it is to *eat,* Father," said Grace with a good-natured look of consciousness.
>
> Uncle Tim tried his best to look sour; but his visage began to wax comical as he looked at his merry daugh-ter; so he said nothing, but quietly sat down to dinner.
>
> "Father," said Grace, after dinner, "we shall want two more candlesticks next week."
>
> "Why, can't you have your party with what you've got?"
>
> "No, Father, we want two more."

"I can't afford it, Grace—there's no sort of use on't—and you sha'n't have any."

"O, Father, now do," said Grace.

"I won't, neither," said Uncle Tim, as he sallied out of the house, and took the road to Comfort Scran's store.

In half an hour he returned again; and fumbling in his pocket, and drawing forth a candlestick, levelled it at Grace.

"There's your candlestick."

"But, Father, I said I wanted *two.*"

"Why, can't you make one do?"

"No, I can't; I must have two."

"Well, then, there's t'other; and here's a fol-de-rol for you to tie round your neck." So saying, he bolted for the door, and took himself off with all speed. It was much after this fashion that matters commonly went on in the brown house.

It is easy enough to criticize the dialogue as trivial, crude, and repetitive, but Uncle Tim emerges from it as a far more than one-dimensional character. He is a New England skinflint, member of a clan recognizable to every nineteenth-century American reader, but he has an individually soft heart that Grace knows how to touch.

Nor is he a stock character. Countless figures like him subsequently appeared in American fiction, but he was totally original as conceived by the author, who relied on qualities, real or popularly imagined, that would enable her readers to recognize what they regarded as a New Englander, a penny-pinching, stubborn figure, whose accent and choice of language were not to be found elsewhere in the United States. For a beginner, the young writer displayed a deft hand and a sure touch.

Once Harriet started to write she could not stop. Here, at last, was the outlet for her frustrations, for her bottled and corked emotions. Her next piece, written in 1833 for the edification of the Semi-Colon Club, as she wrote Georgiana, was "a satire on certain members who were getting very much into the way of joking on the worn-out subjects of matrimony and old maid and old bachelorism." Obviously, Harriet was sensitive on the matter and struck back in the best way she knew. She had the last word, which taught her the power of the pen. Judge Hall liked her vignette and, with slight changes, published it in 1834, paying her his usual fee of fifty dollars for it.

For the Beecher household, 1833 was a busy year. William arrived and, confiding to Hattie that he was being criticized by his congregation for being too frank, asked her advice on the best way to broach the subject to his father. Charles not only became embroiled in violent dinner-table arguments with Lyman Beecher on the subject of Calvinist Jonathan Edwards, the eighteenth-century theologian, whose teachings he repudiated, but dared to hint that he wanted to give up the ministry for a career as a composer of music. Harriet was compelled to intervene to prevent shouting matches.

Mrs. Beecher was ill and was forced to spend much of her time in bed. Harriet, dutiful stepdaughter, waited on her, never admitting what only Henry Ward had ever declared aloud: Papa's second wife was a cold woman who had a passion only for neatness, and thus it was difficult to love her. Edward came for a visit, arriving just in time to help Hattie convince a doubtful George not to abandon the ministry but to remain at Lane until he received his divinity degree the following year. Henry Ward came to Cincinnati, too, enrolling at Lane and surprising the whole family with his new earnestness of purpose. He had flirted with failure throughout his undergraduate career, but the man who would become known as "the greatest oratorical advocate of Christ since Paul" was settling down.

His presence, particularly on a permanent basis, delighted and soothed Harriet. They had seen little of each other in recent years, but quickly drew close again. Henry Ward was the one member of the family with whom she felt completely comfortable, the only one in whom she could confide freely. Less cerebral and more outgoing than most of Lyman Beecher's children, he and Hattie genuinely enjoyed being together because they shared a trait conspicuously lacking in most Beechers, a subtle sense of humor. They could even laugh at themselves, which confounded most members of the family.

Their little sister, Isabella, was jealous of their intimacy, but they paid no attention to her peevish moods, and four decades later they would be haunted by this neglect. When the Great Henry Ward Beecher Scandal, as the press called it, was the sensation of America, Great Britain, and much of western Europe, Isabella was the only member of the family who failed to support Henry Ward, and her brothers and sisters stopped speaking to her. She was prevented from doing his cause material damage by the intervention of Harriet, who had intimidated Isabella since early childhood, just as Harriet herself had been cowed throughout her life by Catherine. No relationships under the roof of the seething Beechers were simple.

It was also in 1833 that Harriet Beecher first became aware of slavery as a living institution. In New England she had politely deplored slavery as an abstraction and re- mained untouched for a time after she and Catherine founded the Western Female Institute, even though two new servants in the Beecher household were black "bound" girls.

But no one who lived in Cincinnati could ignore the challenge of slavery, which existed across the Ohio in Kentucky. Abolitionists were more vehement in the Beechers' newly adopted home city because they saw slavery at close hand, and those who supported the system were more intensely vocal, too. The latter group included cotton brokers, tobacco warehouse owners, and proprietors of river boats, all of whom owed their living to slavery. The largest Underground Railway in the United States, an organization that helped escaped slaves reach safety and freedom in the North, was founded in Cincinnati and operated there until the defeat of the South in the Civil War. It was almost impossible for anyone in Cincinnati to remain neutral on what was rapidly becoming the greatest moral, political, and economic issue of the era.

If Harriet Beecher was relatively tepid in her opinion of slavery for a time, it was only because of her insulation from the outside world. She wrote long letters to Georgiana and Edward about the state of her soul and her relationship to God because that was the primary topic, sometimes the only topic, discussed in Lyman Beecher's house. When writing to sister Mary, Harriet's letters were filled with the trivia of daily existence and bits of family gossip.

It would be unfair to claim that the woman whom Abraham Lincoln later is said to have called "the little lady who started this big war" was unaware in 1833 that Andrew Jackson had begun his second term as President. It is probably a gross exaggeration to state that she was oblivious of the panic of 1837 and its devastating effects on the nation during Martin Van Buren's single term as President. But the unalterable fact remains that in none, of the voluminous correspondence she maintained during her twenties did she mention economic matters, political affairs, or the complexities of government in an increasingly divided nation. It is impossible to guess what was churning in the mind and heart of this woman who had learned to conceal her feelings and who revealed even a little of her inner self only to one or two of her intimates.

There can be no question, however, that what she first saw of slavery made an indelible impression on her. Her curiosity may have been aroused by the strangely passive stand taken by her father. Lyman Beecher was opposed to the institution in principle and was horrified by the brutality of the slave trade, but he thought the abolitionists were taking the wrong approach and in Boston had quarreled publicly with William Lloyd Garrison, the founder of the movement.

Abolitionists, Dr. Beecher said, "are the offspring of the Oneida denunciatory revivals... made up of vinegar, aqua fortis, and oil of vitriol, with brimstone, saltpeter and charcoal to explode and scatter the corrosive matter." He felt that the violence advocated by the abolitionists would cause the South to stiffen in its opposition and that freedom for the slaves would be retarded. Even more important, immediate rather than gradual emancipation would harm the blacks as well as the whites, he believed, since many thousands of slaves were still backward, unable to look after themselves in an advanced civilization. Before being freed they should be educated, and the first step in that process was to make them Christians. Only the Presbyterian Church, he naturally felt, was sufficiently able to achieve this goal.

Whether Harriet completely accepted her father's views is unknown, but, even if she disagreed with him, she had not yet reached the point where she would dare to argue with him in public. All that can be said with certainty is that she wanted to know more about the institution, which could best be accomplished by visiting a working plantation.

In the early autumn of 1833, Samuel Foote made the necessary arrangements. Harriet and a friend, Mary Dutton, a fellow instructor at the institute, crossed the Ohio River by ferry and then rode in a borrowed carriage to an estate owned by one of Samuel's many friends. The place was later depicted in *Uncle Tom's Cabin* as the plantation of Colonel Shelby.

The sheltered young ladies from New England had never seen a farm like it. The fields of corn, hemp, and tobacco were vast, and the blue grass of the lawns looked like a carpet. The house itself had broad verandas and large, high-ceilinged rooms that were sparsely but elegantly furnished with oversized mahogany pieces. Enormous coffee urns and teapots of silver gleamed everywhere.

The young ladies were invited to join the plantation owner and his family in what was described as a "light repast," which they privately thought was a banquet. There were large platters of cold chicken, duck, turkey, and ham. Potatoes and vegetables were heaped in bowls. Biscuits and cornbread were served hot, and there were more butter and cream on the table than the Beecher family used in a week. The servings were so lavish that expense obviously was no consideration. Harriet, who had spent her entire life in genteel poverty, later commented to Mary that such extravagance was sinful.

The mistress of the house was a generous, warmhearted woman, and her husband, although inclined to drink large quantities of wine at the table, was a jovial man who was kind to his slaves. All the same, he required several of them to perform for the entertainment of the guests, much as one would put trained animals through a set of tricks.

The slaves lived in vine-covered log cabins, each with its own small garden, and they seemed happy enough with their lot. From what the visitors could see, none was mistreated. But slaves were still property, no matter how comfortable their living conditions, and could be bought or sold at their owner's whim.

One of the house slaves, lighter skinned than the rest, fascinated the New Englanders. She was a young woman of about their own age, stylishly attired in a snug-fitting dress. The visitors realized she was partly of white ancestry, perhaps a quadroon, and without question the descendant of a white man and a black woman. She was no less a slave because of her paternity, and the callousness of the system sickened the visitors.

Harriet's specific reactions are best described in a letter Mary Dutton wrote many years later. "Hattie did not seem to notice anything in particular that happened, but sat much of the time as though abstracted in thought. When the negroes did funny things and cut up capers, she did not seem to pay the slightest attention to them. Afterwards, however, in reading 'Uncle Tom' I recognized scene after scene of that visit portrayed with the most minute fidelity, and knew at once where the material for that portion of the story had been gathered."

The portrait of a girl, ill at ease and horrified by what she was seeing, gives an intimation of what she would become in another twenty years.

Technical complications had prevented Henry Ward Beecher from receiving his bachelor's degree from Amherst College before he enrolled in the Lane Theological Seminary, so he returned to Massachusetts in the spring of 1834 for the commencement exercises. His favorite sister wanted to attend the ceremonies and followed him in June. It was Harriet's first return to the East after moving to Cincinnati and the first time she had ever traveled alone.

She went by stagecoach to Toledo, then took a steamer as far as Buffalo, where she resumed her overland journey. The highlight of her trip was the sight of Niagara Falls, which so impressed her that she became almost inarticulate when writing about the experience to relatives and friends in Cincinnati. She attended Henry Ward's graduation, visited Georgiana in Hartford, and then went on to Connecticut, for a longer stay with her grandmother.

While there she was upset by the news that her dear friend Eliza Stowe, two years her senior, had died of cholera. She grieved in private and sent Professor Stowe a brief note of condolence.

After Harriet's return to Cincinnati for the beginning of the institute's autumn term, Calvin Stowe was a frequent supper guest at the Beecher house. Harriet had been his late wife's closest friend, and she seemed better able than anyone èlse to offer him the consolation he so badly needed. A brilliant Biblical scholar, he was absentminded in all else. Harriet mended his clothes, saw to it that his boots were polished, had his spectacles repaired, and, when she discovered he sometimes forgot his meals, invited him home more often.

Early in 1835, the second Mrs. Lyman Beecher died after a long illness. Catherine was traveling in the East, recruiting new faculty members and trying to attract bright students, so Harriet not only was in charge of the institute but became acting mistress of her father's household. Calvin Stowe's appearances at the Beecher home became still more frequent.

By the autumn of 1835, Harriet and Professor Stowe began to be seen together in public, and members of the Semi-Colon Club took it for granted that a romance was brewing. At Thanksgiving, to no one's surprise, they announced their engagement, and in January, 1836, they were married.

A belief that sprang up during Harriet Beecher Stowe's lifetime and that has persisted to the present day has it that her relations with her husband during the many years of their marriage were cold and formal. Nothing could be farther from the truth. Possibly the couple's formality with each other in public was the root of the myth. Their habit of addressing each other in public as "Professor Stowe" or "Mr. Stowe" and "Mrs. Stowe" was lifelong, and even their children never saw them kiss or hold hands. Many years after their wedding, Mrs. Stowe freely admitted she had been "wildly in love" with the professor before their marriage and added that her feelings had not changed through the years. They were separated frequently during five decades, sometimes for prolonged periods, and never failed to write each other daily. These communications were filled with terms of endearment, advice, and tender expressions of concern.

Harriet Stowe's fame eclipsed that of her husband, it is true, but Calvin Stowe, despite his naiveté, bumbling ways, and complete inability to handle money, was an emotionally mature man who did not envy his wife's great renown. Before the publication of *Uncle Tom's Cabin,* Calvin Stowe unfailingly encouraged his wife in her career as a writer and thereafter expressed great pride in her success. He was helpless without her and rarely showed any resentment of her management of family affairs.

As they grew older and his health began to fail, he put on a great deal of weight, and this condition undoubtedly hastened his death. Mrs. Stowe sometimes chided him gently, urging him to eat less and become more active, but she never criticized him in front of others. They shared many tragedies, among them the death of one son on the brink of a brilliant career and the mysterious disappearance of another who was making a valiant effort to overcome alcoholism. Their mutual loyalty was unwavering, and their many problems, including the professor's unfortunate tendency to let his wife's money slip through his fingers, did not draw them apart. Fair appraisal makes it possible to draw only one conclusion: Their marriage was solidly successful.

Mrs. Stowe's background and personality were guarantees of her marital fidelity, and it would have been out of character for her to give any other man a second thought. The professor cheerfully admitted that he enjoyed the company of attractive young ladies and liked to look at them, but his mild flirtations were harmless. He, too, was faithful, and, shortly before his death, his wife said he had never given her cause for jealousy, adding that she had the capacity for such feelings.

Nothing better reveals the twenty-five-year-old Harriet Beecher's turbulent state on the day of her wedding than a letter she wrote to Georgiana.

January 6, 1836

Well, my dear G., about half an hour more and your old friend, companion, schoolmate, sister, etc., will cease to be Hattie Beecher and change into nobody knows who. My dear, you are engaged and pledged in a year or two to encounter a similar fate, and do you wish to know how you shall feel? Well, my dear, I have been dreading and dreading the time, and lying awake all last week wondering how I should live through this overwhelming crisis, and lo! it has come and I feel *nothing at all.*

The wedding is to be altogether domestic; nobody present but my own brothers and sisters, and my old colleague, Mary Dutton; and as there is a sufficiency of the ministry in our family we have not even to call in the foreign aid of a minister. Sister Katy is not here, so she will not witness my departure from her care and guidance to that of another. None of my numerous friends and acquaintances who have taken such a deep interest in making the connection for me even know the day, and it will all be done and over before they know anything about it.

Well, it is really a mercy to have this entire stupidity come over one at such a time. I should be crazy to feel as I did yesterday, or indeed to feel anything at all. But I inwardly vowed that my last feelings and reflections on this subject should be yours, and as I have not got any, it is just as well to tell you *that.* Well, here comes Mr. S., so farewell, and for the last time I subscribe

Your own

H. E. B.

Marriage consumed far more of the new Mrs. Stowe's time, thoughts, and energies than she had imagined, and she appears to have forgotten to mail the letter. When she remembered it, she added a postscript, then let additional weeks pass, and did not actually dispatch the letter until two months after the wedding. In the postscript she said:

Three weeks have passed since writing the above, and my husband and self are now quietly seated by our own fireside, as domestic as any pair of tame fowl you ever saw; he writing to his mother, and I to you. Two days after our marriage we took a wedding excursion, so called, though we would most gladly have been excused this conformity to ordinary custom had not necessity required Mr. Stowe to visit Columbus, and I had too much adhesiveness not to go too. Ohio roads at this season are no joke, I can tell you, though we were, on the whole, wonderfully taken care of, and our expedition included as many pleasures as an expedition at this time of year *ever* could.

And now, my dear, perhaps the wonder to you, as to me, is how this momentous crisis in the life of such a wisp of nerves as myself has been transacted so quietly. My dear, it is a wonder to myself. I am tranquil, quiet, and happy. I look *only* on the present, and leave the future with Him who has hitherto been so kind to me. "Take no thought for morrow" is my motto, and my comfort is to rest on Him in whose house there are many mansions provided when these fleeting earthly ones pass away.

Dear Georgy, naughty girl that I am, it is a month that I have let the above lie by, because I got into a strain of emotion in it that I dreaded to return to. Well, so it shall be no longer. In about five weeks Mr. Stowe and myself start for New England. He sails the first of May. I am going with him to Boston, New York, and other places, and shall stop finally at Hartford, whence, as soon as he is gone, it is my intention to turn westward.

Calvin Stowe was traveling to Europe to purchase textbooks for Lane, and, of far greater importance, to undertake a mission on behalf of the state of Ohio. He had been appointed a special commissioner charged with making a study of the public school systems of various nations on the Continent and then making recommendations that would lead to the reorganization of the Ohio school system. This appointment was the outgrowth of his conviction that higher education could not flourish in the West until improvements were made in primary and secondary school education. In 1833 he had been a founder, in Cincinnati, of the College of

Teachers, an institution dedicated to training better teachers and creating a more widespread public demand for education.

The adoption of his recommendations by the state of Ohio resulted in a drastic remodeling of the public schools, and the improvements were widely copied by other states. Stowe's activity won him a measure of renown, at least in American educational circles. He was never the nonentity he was often portrayed as being when his wife became famous.

It is surprising that Professor Stowe failed to take his wife of four months to Europe with him. His expenses were paid by the state, but it is possible they lacked the funds for hers. At any rate, the idea does not seem to have occurred to either, and Mrs. Stowe faced the separation with equanimity, although she did assure her husband in letter after letter, as she urged him to guard his health, that she missed him.

By the time Mrs. Stowe returned to Cincinnati to take up temporary residence under her father's roof, she was pregnant. Unlike many women of the time, she did not go into semiretirement to await the birth of her child but instead plunged into an active life as a writer. She turned out a number of short stories, articles, and essays for the *Western Monthly Magazine* and simultaneously found another outlet for her literary work. Henry Ward had taken a temporary position as editor of a small Cincinnati daily newspaper, the *Journal,* and it soon became a family organ, with Henry Ward himself writing editorials, Charles doing pieces on music, and Mrs. Stowe contributing everything from news stories to special articles. The spring and summer were an exciting time in Cincinnati because two abolitionists established a new magazine which they called the *Philanthropist.* Proslavery mobs were organized and, after burning down the new publication's plant, roamed the city for several days, threatening other institutions.

Henry Ward carried a brace of pistols when he went to work each day, but Mrs. Stowe proved to be fearless when she brought her day's contribution to the *Journal* office, rightly believing that her obvious pregnancy was her protection. Still under their father's influence, brother and sister were convinced that the abolitionists, by advocating violence and thus causing counterviolence, were doing irreparable harm to the antislavery movement. Henry Ward wrote strong editorials on the subject, and Mrs. Stowe prepared a series of satirical articles that held the abolitionists up to ridicule. Peace was not restored to the city until a vigilante force consisting of respectable citizens of all persuasions dispersed the proslavery mobs.

In September, 1837, Mrs. Stowe gave birth to twin daughters. After Professor Stowe's return the following February, the girls were named Eliza Tyler, after his first wife, and Harriet Beecher, after his second.

At about the same time, Lyman Beecher returned from a trip to the Eastern Seaboard, astonishing his children by bringing with him a third wife, the former Mrs. Lydia Jackson, a Boston widow. A competent, brisk woman, she took excellent care of Dr. Beecher in his old age and made it her business to be on good terms with her grown stepchildren, although, years after his death, she tried to obtain money from Mrs. Stowe and Henry Ward Beecher, who were then famous, claiming it was her due for having nursed their father. They thought her demands were outrageous, and broke relations with her.

Mrs. Stowe wrote that her "dowry" consisted of eleven-dollars-worth of dishes and that her husband's principal contribution to their household was his extensive library. Their house was sparsely furnished, and they were too poor to buy more, thanks to the panic of 1837: The contributions on which Lane Theological Seminary depended dwindled alarmingly, and Professor Stowe, when he was paid at all, received only a portion of his salary, He was hopelessly inept at handling family finances, and his wife, inexperienced in running a household, was only somewhat better.

The couple could not afford the services of a hired girl, so Mrs. Stowe did all of the cooking, cleaning, and mending, bought food, and took care of the twins. She loved her husband and children, but she had little talent for the domestic arts. Each week she set firm schedules for herself, only to find that her writing made them meaningless. When the pile of clothes that needed ironing grew high and the kitchen wanted scrubbing, she vowed to stop writing until she finished her chores. But she broke her resolutions as quickly as she made them and continued to do so for the next decade and a half.

The truth of the matter is that nothing could prevent her from writing. The habit of putting words on paper had become compulsive; expressing herself became more important to her than anything else on earth. Bouts of fatigue and other ailments did not stop her, and neither did her later pregnancies.

This is to not to say she neglected her husband or her children. She was an attentive, loving wife who supported her husband's new vocational ventures and his various business schemes. She was a devoted, tender mother, always concerned with the welfare and health of her children. That their clothes sometimes needed mending or pressing, or that she occasionally served the same supper several nights in succession could not be helped. After all, as a professional writer whose income the family badly needed, she had to make the time, when none was readily available, for her work. And no one could blame her if ideas crowded her mind more rapidly than she could scribble them on long sheets of cheap foolscap. She was paid an average of two dollars per page for her labors, and could turn out a page in a quarter of an hour, or less.

Mrs. Stowe wisely used her first earnings to hire a maid-of-all-work, and her burden was eased slightly. By the late spring of 1837, the depression had deepened, however, and the professor's salary payments became even more sporadic. She admired Henry Ward. He had just been ordained and, after marrying a girl named Eunice Bullard, had gone with her to live in Lawrenceburg, Ohio, on an income of $400 per year. Her brother and new sister-in-law, Mrs. Stowe said, had far more courage than she possessed, and she wished she dared attempt to live on so little.

So difficult was it for her to make ends meet that at one time she decided to resort to the stratagem commonly adopted by those living in genteel poverty: taking in boarders. Stowe discouraged her, pointing out that she would earn far less than she was making from her writing and that their privacy would be destroyed. Catherine intervened, too, and with her customary forcefulness persuaded Mrs. Stowe to abandon her idea. Anyone who earned two dollars per page for writing was foolish to contemplate taking on any other sort of work.

So Mrs. Stowe made strenuous efforts to find new markets, and not only made inquiries of fellow members of the Semi-Colon Club but wrote to various friends in Hartford, too. The strain was too much for her nervous system, especially because in the summer of 1837 she was pregnant again. The professor became alarmed at her declining health and insisted she take a holiday from family responsibilities. Despite misgivings, she obediently went for a visit at the home of William and his wife in Putnam, Ohio.

There she received heavy exposure to the abolitionist cause. William had become active in the movement, his wife shared his enthusiasm, and friends who came to visit spoke of little else. Mrs. Stowe hated idleness and spent hours each day reading abolitionist tracts. For the first time, they made sense to her, she admitted years later, and she became convinced that slavery was so evil it had to be destroyed. She still abhorred violence, however, and by now she knew enough to realize the economy of the South depended on the institution. No man would give up his living without a struggle, and the drastic means advocated by the abolitionists were certain to create equally violent countermeasures. She agreed that slavery had to be abolished and that it made a mockery of the principles for which the United States claimed it stood. The best way to be rid of it, she believed, was through a process of education that would better enable North and South to understand each other. Only if that method failed would more direct means be justified.

She was willing to grant that delay served the cause of slave owners, that hundreds of thousands of men, women, and children would remain in bondage during the years that would pass before an educational campaign could take effect. But this slow procedure would better serve the cause of justice in the long run, she declared, remembering the ugly rioting of the proslavery mobs she had seen in Cincinnati. "It does seem to me," she wrote, "that there needs to be an *intermediate* society. If not, as light increases, all the excesses of the abolitionist party will not prevent humane and conscientious men from joining it."

Mrs. Stowe returned home in the autumn, and late in January, 1838, she gave birth to her third child, Henry Ellis. Catherine thought the baby should be named after his grandfather, but Mrs. Stowe insisted on giving him the name of her favorite brother.

A few months later, there was a reunion of all the Beechers. Edward brought Mary with him on his return from a trip to the East, and George came from Batavia, New York, where he had his congregation. Never had Lyman Beecher been as happy as he was on Sunday, when his pulpit was filled by Edward in the morning, William in the afternoon, and George in the evening.

In 1839 Mrs. Stowe hired a black girl form Kentucky as her family's servant. Under the laws of Ohio, the girl was free, having been brought into the state and left there by her mistress, but one day Professor Stowe learned that her master had come to Cincinnati from Kentucky and was searching for her. He and Henry Ward immediately armed themselves and then spirited the girl to the farm of a friend who lived about twelve miles from the city; she remained there in hiding until the danger passed. Mrs. Stowe later recalled every detail of the incident, and used the story in *Uncle Tom's Cabin* when she described the flight of the fugitives.

By the early 1840s, Mrs. Stowe was writing furiously for a number of magazines. During a trip to the East she paid a visit to the offices of the *New York Evangelist,* one of the more moderate abolitionist publications, and the editors agreed to accept both fiction and nonfiction from her. She made a similar arrangement with a new magazine with intellectual pretensions, *Souvenir,* published in Cincinnati.

The editor of the *Boston Miscellany* promised to do better than the others, offering her twenty dollars for every three pages of her copy that he published. But an agreement was never reached. Her fellow author Edward Everett Hale was the authority for the statement that Mrs. Stowe was shocked by a fashion illustration in the *Miscellany* portraying a woman in a very low-cut dress, and refused to allow her name to be associated with such an enterprise.

Instead, she began to write for the most prestigious and popular of all women's magazines of the period, *Godey's Lady's Book,* and thousands of subscribers read her work. Nothing could be farther from the truth than the story that she was an unknown amateur writer when *Uncle Tom's Cabin* startled the world.

Her subject matter came from her own surroundings. A strong plea for temperance reflected Lyman Beecher's sermons. Too many fine ladies and gentlemen were serving wine at their dinner tables, forgetting that the fermented juice of the grape was fatal to the weak-willed. And in this case it was wrong to mind one's own business, since it was the obligation of every good Christian to act as his brother's keeper. She wrote two personal pieces, one on Henry Ward, once almost inarticulate, who was rapidly developing into "a silver-tongued preacher second to none," the other a description of a night she had spent on a canal boat. Two others grew from reflection on feminine concerns: an article on the heartlessness of wealthy women who paid starvation wages to their seamstresses and a study of the servant problem in the United States. Since there was no true servant class in America, the efficient worker moved upward into the mainstream of society. As a consequence, American ladies were frequently forced to train new servants or to accept the help of the inefficient. In a tract on the keeping of the Sabbath, Mrs. Stowe expressed a longing for the strict observance she had known in her Litchfield childhood. Unnamed Cincinnati neighbors were courting disaster by sleeping late on Sundays, sending their children off to religious instruction without adequate preparation, and otherwise failing to keep the Sabbath day holy. In so doing, she warned, they were guaranteeing their future misery, for only through the acquisition of spiritual qualities could people attain true happiness.

Her fiction was romantic, the settings always centered on rural and small-town New England. Her usual technique was to base the story on a single memorable character, more often than not an elderly man endowed with marked personality quirks. She rarely set her scenes in Cincinnati or smaller Ohio towns in spite of her familiarity with them.

By 1842 she had published a large body of work, broad enough in scope for her to open negotiations with the Harper brothers of New York, who agreed to publish a collection of her New England short stories under the collective title *The Mayflower*. She received an advance royalty payment of $100, and in the next decade the book earned an additional $500. A new printing immediately following publication of *Uncle Tom's Cabin* earned thousands, and in 1855 a revised edition of the stories appeared. By this time her fame was so great that its overnight success was ensured.

During this period of hard, successful work, family matters continued to distract Mrs. Stowe. Her mother-in-law came to Cincinnati for a visit in 1838 and remained for the better part of a year. The elder Mrs. Stowe was well meaning but incapable of allowing another woman to manage her own household. Her interference was a never ending source of annoyance, but Harriet Stowe, who so often preached patience, had ample opportunity to take her own advice, and the two women parted on good terms.

In the late spring of 1839, Professor Stowe went East to deliver a Phi Beta Kappa oration at Dartmouth College and took his wife and children with him. While he busied himself with academic matters and a friend looked after the youngsters for a few days, his wife took a side trip through the White Mountains, later turning her familiarity with the scenic background to good effect in several books.

Late in the year, Mrs. Stowe was pregnant again, and in May, 1840, she gave birth to her fourth child, a son. He was named Frederick William because, she wrote Georgiana, the professor greatly admired the King of Prussia, a man who reputedly cultivated self-discipline in all of his relationships. Stowe had met him several years earlier, when studying the public school systems of European nations.

Two years later, while Mrs. Stowe was making one of her periodic visits to Hartford, the Prussian Ambassador paid a visit to Cincinnati and called at the Stowe's house to tell the professor how pleased King Frederick William had been with his report on Prussian schools.

Of far greater importance to the academician, however, was his wife's absence from home, and an excerpt from a letter he sent indicates his dependence on her.

> And now, my dear wife, I want you to come home as quick as you can. The fact is I cannot live without you, and if we were not so prodigious poor I would come for you at once. There is no woman like you in this wide world. Who else has so much talent with so little self-conceit; so much reputation with so little affectation; so much literature with so little nonsense; so much enterprise with so little extravagance; so much tongue with so little scold; so much sweetness with so little softness; so much of so many things and so little of so many other things?

Echoing his sentiments, Mrs. Stowe replied:

> I was telling Belle yesterday that I did not know till I came away how much I was dependent upon you for information. There are a thousand favorite subjects on which I could talk with you better than with any one else. If you were not already my dearly loved husband I should certainly fall in love with you.

The Stowes were reunited at the end of the summer of 1842, and that winter long remained in their memories. An epidemic of typhoid fever struck Cincinnati, and so many of the seminary students were stricken that Dr. Beecher had to convert his home into a temporary hospital.

In July, 1843, a few weeks before the birth of Mrs. Stowe's third daughter, Georgiana May, she and the rest of the family were shocked by the death of George Beecher. Unfamiliar with firearms, which he ordinarily refrained from using because his wife loathed them, he nevertheless took a shotgun into the orchard behind his parsonage to get rid of birds that were eating his fruit. He killed himself, and, because there were no witnesses, it was later rumored that he had committed suicide. It is true that his moods were as intense as those suffered by his sister Harriet, but no verifiable basis has ever been found for the allegation.

Mrs. Stowe grieved, as did all the Beechers, and soon thereafter a new note crept into her correspondence with Hartford and Boston friends. She still felt an alien in Ohio after living there for a decade, and she dreamed of returning to her own New England.

The death of George Beecher marked the beginning of a bleak period in the lives of the Stowes, a time of seemingly endless misery when even their faith in the Almighty failed to sustain them. By the autumn of 1843, Lane Seminary was on the verge of collapse, and Mrs. Stowe revealed in her correspondence that her husband was being paid only half of his $1,200 annual salary. In the spring of 1844, the school's situation was so desperate that Professor Stowe made a trip East in an atttempt to raise funds. His wife, inundated by family responsibilities and trying to find time for her own necessary work as a writer, revealed her state of mind when she told him in a letter: "I am already half sick with confinement to the house and overwork. If I should sew every day for a month to come I should not be able to accomplish a half of what is to be done, and should be only more unfit for my other duties."

For month after weary month, she struggled with domestic chores, tried to stretch her husband's inadequate income, and then stayed up late at night to write the stories and magazine articles that put food on the family table. By the late spring of 1845, she was near the breaking point and wrote her husband, who was attending a convention of ministers in Detroit, "I am sick of the smell of sour milk, and sour meat, and sour everything, and then the clothes *will* not dry, and no wet thing does, and everything smells mouldy; and altogether I feel as if I never wanted to eat again."

In spite of her troubles, her writing never faltered, and she returned repeatedly to the theme of slavery, which was beginning to haunt her. In a short story called "Immediate Emancipation," which appeared in the January, 1845, issue of the *New York Evangelist,* she revealed her preoccupation with one aspect of the problem. A slave, treated with kindness by his master, nevertheless is terror-stricken, deathly afraid the day will come when he will be sold to pay his master's debts. On one memorable occasion, near the Cincinnati waterfront, Mrs. Stowe had seen a slave family torn apart, the father sold to one buyer, the mother to another, and their three-year-old child left without parents. Unable to tolerate the injustice, Mrs. Stowe borrowed the money to buy the child and was able to reunite her with her mother. But thousands of slaves were being similarly treated like cattle, and there seemed to be nothing that an impoverished housewife and part-time writer of minor words could do to help them.

The situation was not relieved by a growing schism in the Presbyterian church. The conservative faction, which was beginning to make excuses for slavery, had long been opposed to Lyman Beecher on theological grounds and now actively sought his dismissal from the seminary as a radical. Dr. Beecher and his sons replied by taking a firmer antislavery stand, but the old man was sufficiently charitable toward his enemies to declare that, as ministers, they were performing good works.

His children did not turn the other cheek. Henry Ward, who had moved to a fine church in Indianapolis, where proslavery sentiment was strong, jeopardized his new post by exercising his rapidly developing oratorical skills in ringing denunciations of slavery. William's abolitionist activities cost him his pastorate in Putnam, and Edward, who had become the head of a new school, Illinois College, located in the southern part of that state, where there were strong proslavery advocates, made so many enemies that he felt compelled to give up his post.

Mrs. Stowe came to believe her antislavery writing efforts were an insufficient expression of her growing zeal for the cause. A colony of former slaves lived on property leased from Lane Seminary, and when she discovered their children completely lacked educational benefits she gave up a portion of her own precious time to act as their teacher and to recruit others to perform the same task.

She learned a great deal about the inner workings of the system from her new cook and maid-of-all-work, Eliza Buck, a former slave. Horrified when she was told that all of the woman's children had been sired by her former master, she could not put one sentence of the explanation out of her mind: "You know, Mrs. Stowe, slave women cannot help themselves."

Equally unsettling was the woman's revelation of actual conditions that Mrs. Stowe previously had believed to be the figment of abolitionist propaganda. Field workers on Louisiana plantations, the former slave told her, were driven with whips and subjected to severe beatings if they failed to fulfill their quotas. Those who dared to protest against such brutality were whipped until they lost consciousness and left to lie in the fields as an additional punishment. Other slaves often crept out of their cabins late at night to help their suffering comrades, risking beatings if they were caught.

It has been suggested that Mrs. Stowe found an outlet for the frustrations in her own life in her opposition to slavery, but this need not necessarily have been the case. She and other members of the Beecher family became increasingly aware of the problems and injustice created by the institution as waves of moral indignation mounted year by year in the North, and their reactions were typical of those of millions of others. During her first years in Cincinnati, Harriet Beecher Stowe had been a moderate on the issue. By the mid-1840s, however, her outrage was simmering, as was that of other members of her family, and soon would reach the boiling point. Certainly, Henry Ward suffered few frustrations during this time, but his anger was rising, too. It may be assumed that Mrs. Stowe would have been no less indignant over the slave system had she already achieved great sucess as a writer or had her husband regularly received his full salary. No Beecher ever shrank from a moral cause.

Lyman Beecher, in spite of his enemies, was riding high. In 1846 he was sent on a lecture tour of England by the Christian Alliance, with temperance as his principal topic, and one of his talks, at Covent Garden, was attended by Queen Victoria. He was asked so many questions about the slavery issue that he sometimes departed from his text to trace the history of the abolitionist movement, and he predicted that the days of slavery in the United States were numbered.

Dr. Beecher's third daughter had no opportunity to share in the family celebrations of her father's triumph. Late in the summer of 1845, a cholera epidemic struck Cincinnati, and Mrs. Stowe, already debilitated by overwork, fell gravely ill. The physicians summoned by Professor Stowe could do nothing for her, and it appeared so likely she would die that her husband, her father, and her brothers took turns praying over her in a vigil that lasted for three days and nights.

She passed the crisis but was greatly weakened, and recovery was painfully slow. She remained feeble for the rest of the year, lacking the strength to write and unable to perform her duties as a wife, mother, and housekeeper. By early 1846, it appeared she might be an invalid for the rest of her life, but Catherine Beecher refused to contemplate such a calamity.

Catherine had great faith in a Dr. Wesselhoeft, who owned and operated a health spa in Brattleboro, Vermont. One of Catherine's friends had been subjected to his regimen, which consisted of alternating "wave baths" and "sitz baths" in waters from a mineral spring, and had been cured of various ailments. Insisting that Mrs. Stowe go to the spa, Catherine enlisted the aid of Mary, and her two sisters accompanied Harriet there, themselves taking the treatment for a short period.

Mrs. Stowe submitted to Dr. Wesselhoeft's ministrations with good grace, but her progress was so slow that for months it was almost imperceptible. She was forced to remain in Brattleboro until the end of the year, leaving her husband to cope with children, house, and financial problems unaided. She remained so weak and listless that not until November, about a month prior to her departure, did her energies revive sufficiently for her to resume her writing.

She arrived home early in January, 1847, her health seemingly better than it had been in years, and immediately resumed her responsibilities, which included spending several hours each day at her writing desk. A year after her return to Cincinnati, in January, 1848, Mrs. Stowe gave birth to her third son, Samuel Charles.

It is fascinating to note that, with the exception of abolitionism, virtually no occurrence or issue of significance in the nation or world appears to have touched Mrs. Stowe's consciousness in the 1840s. Texas declared its independence from Mexico, fought a war to achieve that goal, and was admitted to the Union. The United States fought its own war with Mexico, and the spoils of victory included the acquisition of vast territories that extended the Republic's boundaries to the Pacific Ocean. The California Gold Rush was one of the most dramatic mass migrations in history. But Mrs. Stowe lived in splendid insulation, concerning herself with her husband, children, and home and with her writing of short stories and articles dealing with domestic matters. Anything that her father, brothers, and sisters did was of vital interest to her, but beyond her limited circle she pondered only the will of God and became increasingly indignant over the atrocities, real and alleged, committed by slave owners in the South. It is ironic that this woman who saw so little beyond her own fireside should have become a powerful influence, in her own right, in the determination of the course of American history.

By 1849 the sons of Lyman Beecher by his first wife had acquired comfortable livings. William's congregation was in Batavia, New York; Edward had resettled in Boston; Henry Ward was making a name for himself in Brooklyn, New York; and Charles, whose advanced, pragmatic theological views ultimately would cause him to break with the Presbyterian church, had a pastorate in Fort Wayne, Indiana. Their younger half brothers had not yet become ministers. Thomas, whose love of all things mechanical made him wish he had become an inventor, was teaching school in Hartford, and James had gone to sea, having last written to his family from Indian Ocean ports.

Mrs. Stowe had little opportunity to revel in her brothers' improving fortunes. The health of her husband, who had held his family together during her absence, broke in June, 1848, and it was his turn to go to Brattleboro to take the healing water. He remained at the spa until the autumn of the following year.

During his absence, his wife, now in her late thirties, worked furiously to support herself and six children, Professor Stowe's income having been completely cut off when he fell ill. She was also responsible for paying for his treatment. Assisted by one servant she not only kept house for her family but took in boarders. At night, after the children went to bed, she wrote furiously, churning out a never ending stream of stories and articles, for which she was paid the usual two dollars per page. She also managed to write cheerful daily letters to her husband and kept up her voluminous correspondence with various friends.

She suffered from no physical or emotional ailments during this trying period. In fact, her health was better than it had been at any time since childhood. She confessed in a letter to Henry Ward and his wife that she always felt tired, but added, "My eyesight has improved and I've had no headaches. I have no *time* for such luxuries at present."

In the summer of 1849, a new and serious epidemic of cholera broke out in Cincinnati. Professor Stowe, worried about his family, wanted to come home, but his wife was very firm, telling him there was nothing he could do to protect the children and that he would only expose himself to the disease.

Soon thereafter, two of the children were stricken with cholera, Henry, the eldest son, and Samuel Charles, the youngest. Both boys began to recover, but the family dog died very suddenly, and Mrs. Stowe, who had few superstitions, was worried. A few days later, her worst fears were realized when the baby took a turn for the worse and nothing could be done to save him. "The hand of the Lord hath touched us," the heartbroken mother wrote to her husband.

In September, 1849, Professor Stowe came home at last, bringing welcome news. Bowdoin College, in Brunswick, Maine, had offered him a distinguished-service professorship in "Natural and Revealed Religion." Mrs. Stowe's joy was tempered when she learned the post would pay only $1,000 per year and that the family would be forced to rent a house at a cost of $75 to $100 per year. The situation was complicated by the reaction of the Lane trustees, who promptly gave Stowe an increase in salary to $1,500 per year; almost simultaneously, too, he received an offer from New York of $2,300 per year.

Neither he nor his wife gave serious consideration to the idea of going to New York. It was too large, bustling, and expensive for their tastes, and Mrs. Stowe had disliked it since her first visit there. She was eager to leave Cincinnati and return to the New England she loved, so she rationalized, saying that food, clothing, and other living expenses would be cheaper in a small Maine town than in a large city. But the cost of making the move and settling in a new home would not be cheap, so at her instigation Calvin Stowe wrote to Bowdoin, saying he would accept if they would also give him a cash grant of $500. They agreed, and the matter was settled.

The professor felt honor-bound to remain at Lane until a successor was found, so the family spent the winter of 1849-50 in Cincinnati. Mrs. Stowe became impatient, and it was arranged that she would leave for Brunswick in April, taking three of the children with her, finding a suitable house, and moving in. Her husband would follow with the other two children as soon as he could leave.

The family was drifting eastward again, and Mrs. Stowe's farewell to her seventy-five-year-old father was cheerful. He, too, would return to New England when he retired in the near future. En route to Maine, she stopped for a visit with Henry Ward in Brooklyn and was delighted by his rapid progress. His salary had been increased to a handsome $3,300 per year, he was provided with a comfortable parsonage at no cost, and his congregation had just made him the gift of a carriage worth $600.

After pausing for a week in Hartford with Mary and Isabella, she traveled next to Boston, where she spent several days with Edward and his family, and she found that he, too, was eminently successful. Beechers expanded and grew in the air of their native New England, and Mrs. Stowe's expectations were high, her spirits buoyant in spite of the tiring jouney.

She was careful of her expenses on the trip, writing to the professor that, between Cincinnati and Brunswick, she had spent only $66. A charming house selected by a friend awaited her, and she intended to spend $150 for necessary furnishings. Her earnings from her writing in the next year would enable them to make additional purchases. Soon after her arrival, her dear friend Georgiana May Sykes came for a visit, and they celebrated Mrs. Stowe's thirty-ninth birthday by taking an invigorating walk in nearby pine woods.

There was much to be done to put the new house—musty and cold after being empty for several years—in working order. Mrs. Stowe was upset by gloomy letters from her husband: His funds were exhausted, his health was poor, and he doubted that he would live long enough to join her. Her cheerful reply made light of his fears. His spirits would improve when he reached Maine; one of her publishers was sending her a substantial sum of money in the immediate future; and in any event the Lord would provide, as he always did.

Professor Stowe's pessimistic prophecy was not fulfilled, and he reached Brunswick early in July. The following week his wife, who had made no complaint about traveling with three small children and settling in a new house when in an advanced state of pregnancy, gave birth to another son. He was named Charles after the baby who had died of cholera and thirty-six years later Charles Edward Stowe would win his own crumbs of immortality by writing his mother's official biography.

The family thoroughly enjoyed the summer, going on

numerous outings and picnics, but as autumn approached the spirits of the adults began to droop. The vacation was ended, and Professor Stowe had to return to Cincinnati for yet another year of teaching, the arrival of his successor having been delayed. All of the children remained behind with their mother, and Mrs. Stowe faced some hard facts. Principal among them was the realization that she and her husband faced certain bankruptcy unless she wrote incessantly. Their expenses ran at least three hundred dollars more than the salary her husband was still earning at Lane, and even though times were better they still lived in dread that he might receive only a portion of what was due him.

Winter comes early in Maine, and, with the snow thick on the ground, in November, 1850, Mrs. Stowe's first problem was that of finding a suitable place to write. She finally settled on the parlor because the largest fireplace was located there, and as a desk she used a gateleg table that served an ornamental purpose during the daytime.

Now, as she began to write, she discovered there was only one subject in her mind: the new law passed by Congress that made it mandatory for citizens in the North to return escaped slaves to their owners in the South. This provision was part of the Omnibus Bill of 1850 engineered by Senators Henry Clay and Daniel Webster, the latter regarded as a traitor by the abolitionists, whose ranks more than quadrupled overnight. Signed into law by President Millard Fillmore on September 20, the bill, a compromise effort intended to mollify both North and South in the growing dispute over slavery, was regarded by many of its foes as an outright betrayal of principle. The bill also admitted California to the Union as a free-soil state. The rest of the region acquired from Mexico was to be divided at the thirty-seventh parallel into two territories, Utah and New Mexico, and the question of whether they would be slave or free was carefully ignored. Texas, a slave state, received $10 million in compensation for land it lost in the creation of the New Mexico Territory. The slave trade, but not slavery itself, was banned in the District of Columbia. And the laws regarding the return of fugitive slaves were tightened.

The Beechers were up in arms. Henry Ward electrified his congregation when he introduced a runaway slave from his pulpit and without further ado raised the money to purchase the man and give him his immediate freedom. Edward and his wife openly defied the new law, as did many others, and announced that they were active participants in the Underground Railway that helped runaway slaves escape to Canada.

Mrs. Stowe immediately joined in the struggle, too. Edward Beecher's wife was right in urging her to write, and write, and write. She would not only earn the money to eliminate her family's financial deficit, but would make her contribution to the fight against an immoral, cruel, and inhumane law that made a mockery of the justice on which American civilization theoretically was built.

7

"Now, Hattie, if I could use a pen as you can," Mrs. Edward Beecher wrote to her sister-in-law in late September, 1850, "I would write something that would make this whole nation feel what an accursed thing slavery is." That challenge was directly responsible for the creation of *Uncle Tom's Cabin*, although Mrs. Stowe received other stimuli, too, before she began to write the book that intensified antislavery sentiment in the North and hardened the South's resistance to change. Other members of the family urged her to take a more active role in the cause, and the editor of the *National Era*, a new abolitionist magazine, offered practical encouragement.

Since early 1849, Mrs. Stowe had sent occasional short articles to the *National Era*, which was published in Washington, D.C., by an old acquaintance, Gamaliel Bailey, whose printing presses in Cincinnati had been destroyed by a proslavery mob. In the summer of 1850, he published a short story she had sent him, "The Freeman's Dream," and his readers responded with such enthusiasm that he asked for more in a similar vein. At the time, Mrs. Stowe could think of no suitable fiction, however, and instead contributed several antislavery articles to the *New York Evangelist,* each more vehement than the last.

Late in the autumn of 1850, Bailey, who had great faith in her talents and believed she would surpass all of her previous efforts, took the unprecedented step of sending her a check for $100 and asked her to write a new antislavery story for him. Mrs. Stowe tried to oblige, but her mind remained blank. Never before had she been at a loss for ideas for such a long time. She sat before the fire night after night, staring into the flames, but inspiration appeared to have deserted her.

One cold Sunday morning in February, 1851, as Mrs. Stowe attended Communion services at the college chapel, a vision suddenly filled her mind. She saw an old slave being subjected to a viciously brutal beating, while his tormentor was urged to further excesses by another white man. Then the scene changed, and she saw the dying slave forgive his murderers as he prayed for the salvation of their souls.

For the rest of her life, Mrs. Stowe was convinced that the Almighty had reached out to her, that the inspiration had been His, not her own. Even had she known of the workings of the unconscious mind, it is improbable that she would have accepted any other explanation. As far back as she could remember, her father had preached that miracles were very real, and she accepted his word as fact. Now she knew he had told the truth, because she had been instrumental in the working of a miracle.

She hurried home from church and, dinner forgotten, put her vision on paper, describing the scenes precisely as she had seen them. Overcome by emotion, she summoned her hungry children and read aloud what she had written. All of them wept, and one sobbed, "Oh, Mama! Slavery is the most cruel thing in the world." Any doubts about the work she still may have entertained were swept aside at that moment.

Mrs. Stowe decided she would not write a short story but would dedicate herself to a far more ambitious project, a full-length novel. She would write it in installments, a practice of the period followed by the great Charles Dickens and many others, with each installment a virtually complete story.

Mrs. Stowe realized that a fictional attack on slavery had to be based on fact if it were to accomplish its purpose: She could not draw only on her imagination. Until now, her research for her short articles and stories, including the acquisition of background material, had either been her own experience or based on bits of information she had gleaned from others. Now, however, she needed a great deal more in order to accomplish her goal.

First, she read everything available in her own house. In a magazine for children published by Bailey, *A Friend of Youth,* she found a harrowing account of an escaping slave making her way in mid-winter across Ohio River ice floes. All at once, still guided by inspiration, she remembered the quadroon slave girl she had seen years before on her visit to the Kentucky plantation, and at that moment one of the book's most effective and dramatic scenes was born, the escape of Eliza across the ice. Stories that Eliza Buck had told her about the New Orleans slave market came to mind, too, and the overall design of her book began to take shape.

Her thirst for additional factual data was insatiable. She inaugurated an extensive correspondence with a former slave who had become famous in Europe as well as in the United States as an abolitionist orator and editor: Frederick Douglass, the son of a slave woman and a white father. Knowledge of the day-to-day existence of those in bondage was not enough; she needed to know the innermost thoughts and feelings of slaves.

When the weather became warmer and the roads opened, Mrs. Stowe went to Boston, where the delighted Edward Beechers offered her all the help they could muster. There she learned in full detail the stories of two former slaves: Lewis Clark, who had lived for a long time with Mrs. Beecher's family, and the Reverend Josiah Henson. Clark, an octoroon often assumed to be white, had escaped from the South under dramatic circumstances, and she created a character like him for the husband of the quadroon, Eliza. Clark's sister, Delia, had a romantic history that was perfect for a nineteenth-century novelist's purposes. Placed on the New Orleans block by a vicious master, she had been bought by a Frenchman who had freed her, married her, lived happily with her in the West Indies and France, and left her a fortune when he died.

Henson, founder of a colony of fugitive slaves in Canada, convert to Christianity, and good friend of the Edward Beechers, had given up a chance to escape from slavery in order to care for the sick son of his master, and, not until much later, after saving the child's life, did he make good his escape. Certainly, Mrs. Stowe felt, like the man in her vision, Henson must have forgiven his oppressors.

There were many books about slavery in Edward Beecher's library, and what he did not own he obtained for his sister from the abolitionist headquarters in Boston. Mrs. Stowe was horrified by the notorious *Code Noir of Louisiana* and later said she kept a copy on her desk throughout the preparation of her book. She also found quantities of useful data in a legal pamphlet by a Judge Stroud of Philadelphia that analyzed the laws relating to slavery in each of the Southern states.

The Life of Frederick Douglass, perhaps the most widely read of abolitionist books, was of great use to Mrs. Stowe, as was *Slavery as It Is*, by Theodore Weld, a man her father had attacked from his pulpit as an abolitionist with violent incendiary views. She obtained still more information from the popular works of Richard H. Dana, Jr., and from a number of books of observation and travel written by Northerners who had visited the South.

Late in March, 1851, Mrs. Stowe received a letter from Bailey telling her the *National Era* was being converted from a monthly to a weekly magazine and asking whether she could provide him with a portion of her story each week. In April she sent him the opening chapter, together with a brief note saying she would comply.

The first chapter appeared in the magazine in May under a title provided by Bailey, "Uncle Tom's Cabin; or, the Man That Was a Thing." Each week Mrs. Stowe sent the editor another chapter, believing the work would be completed in six months or less. But, like her character Topsy, the story grew and grew and was not finished until March, 1852, after a full year of unremitting effort. The last chapter ran in serial form in April of that year, but the complete book was published on March 20.

During the long months of writing—and for the rest of her life—Mrs. Stowe remained convinced she had written a moderate work, consonant with her religion and the teachings of her father. Her Kentucky family, the Shelbys, were kind and civilized and treated their slaves with compassion. But they, like the slaves themselves, were victims of the institution itself, and it was that institution, its injustices magnified by the cruelties of the cold-blooded, inhumane slave trade, that she sought to expose and destroy.

In a truly Christian world, she believed, slavery could not exist. Its perpetuation was partly the fault of the churches, including the conservative wing of the Presbyterian movement. These organizations had lost sight of two basic tenets: that God's love is all-pervasive and that man redeems himself through Christ. Instead of practicing religion, they had allowed themselves to become enmeshed in hair-splitting theological arguments, while the wicked and the evils they perpetrated flourished.

At no time did the author's common sense desert her. Her slave-owner characters, in the main, are decent, honorable people, themselves victims of the institution of slavery and more commendable than the abolitionists who advocated any means, no matter how violent, to rid the nation of a curse. More radical antislavery elements in the country, she predicted in her correspondence, would be "sorely disappointed" by her book and might even regard her as a traitor to their cause.

She was also concerned with what would become of the former slaves should immediate, complete emancipation be granted. No longer would there be a place for them on the plantations of the South. Illiterate, without the skills that would enable them to work in factories, they would not be at home in the rapidly industrializing North either, particularly as most Northern citizens, despite their professed antislavery sentiments, were showing no tendency to admit blacks into their homes, their schools, or even their churches. To send all the freed slaves to Liberia, a plan advocated by many abolitionists, struck her as absurd: Their only hope for the future lay on the road to Christianity, and in Africa they would revert to heathenism. Though Mrs. Stowe's opposition to slavery had hardened, she still clung to the opinion that gradual emancipation achieved through religion and education provided the only genuine solution. The economy of the South would be disrupted when the slaves departed, and gradual emancipation was the only fair way to protect plantation owners, who would need time to find other sources of labor.

Apparently unable to assess the intensity of feeling in both North and South, Mrs. Stowe believed that in writing her book she was performing a healing function. Extremists might hate her, but *Uncle Tom's Cabin* would surely appeal to moderates in both sections of the country; when they banded together, slavery could be destroyed in the manner least harmful to everyone concerned.

"I could not control the story; it wrote itself," Mrs. Stowe said a few years after its publication. "I the author of *Uncle Tom's Cabin*? No, indeed. The Lord Himself wrote it, and I was but the humblest of instruments in His hand. To Him alone should be given all the praise." These are not expressions of false modesty. She meant every word. Since God was love, not only would her book help rid America of slavery, it would be an active force in reconciling North and South.

Serialization of *Uncle Tom's Cabin* brought Mrs. Stowe the sum of $300, precisely what she needed to make ends meet. It created such a stir that several book publishers became interested in the work, among them John P. Jewett of Boston, who owned one of the most modern power-operated printing presses in the United States. He offered Mrs. Stowe a 50 percent interest in the profits, provided she also shared the expenses.

Uncertain what to do, she turned to her husband for advice. Professor Stowe promptly opened correspondence with Jewett himself, saying he and his wife were too poor to take any risks. The publisher replied by offering a royalty payment of 10 percent of the retail price, and Stowe accepted on his wife's behalf.

The contract was signed on March 13, 1852, and the first copies of the book, now known as *Uncle Tom's Cabin; or, Life Among the Lowly*, appeared one week later. The first printing consisted of five thousand copies, and the clothbound edition sold for fifty-six cents. In an attempt to promote *Uncle Tom's Cabin*, Mrs. Stowe sought the support of prominent anti-slavery leaders in England and sent prepublication copies to Prince Albert, the Duke of Argyll, Lords Shaftesbury and Carlisle, and several other noblemen. She also sent copies to such distinguished colleagues as Charles Dickens, Thomas Babbington Macaulay, and Charles Kingsley, the most renowned clergyman-author of his day. All replied with courtesy, interest, and sympathy.

No one, least of all Mrs. Stowe, was prepared for the reaction of the American public to *Uncle Tom's Cabin*. Perhaps no other book in publishing history ever created so great a sensation. Three thousand copies were sold the first day, a second edition was published the next week, and a third appeared on April 1. In less than a year 120 editions were printed, with total sales of more than three hundred fifty thousand. An English publisher, Sampson, Low and Company, tried to keep up with the demand in Great Britain by bringing out forty different editions, the cheapest selling for sixpence a copy, the most expensive, an illustrated edition, for forty shillings. Within two years, the book was also published in French, Spanish, Danish, Finnish, Dutch, Flemish, Polish, Russian, Bohemian, Hungarian, Serbian, Armenian, Illyrian, Romaic, Wallachian, Welsh, and Siamese. Ultimately, it was published in forty languages.

Its total sales were astronomical. During the fifty-eight years that Mrs. Stowe and her heirs held copyrights, between three and four million copies were sold in the United States, with more than one and a half million copies selling in Great Britain and four million in foreign translations. No accurate figures are available for copies printed since the expiration of copyrights, but the book has continued to be published in the United States and throughout the world to the present day.

A scant four months after the Boston publication, Mrs. Stowe received her first royalty check, for $10,000, as much as her husband would earn in a decade, assuming he ever actually came to Bowdoin College. Now forty-one years old, she was stunned by this first in a seemingly endless series of windfalls. She hired a cook and a housemaid, but otherwise did not immediately change her style of living.

Had she wished, Mrs. Stowe could have doubled or tripled her income from *Uncle Tom's Cabin*. In the summer of 1852, she received a letter from Asa Hutchinson, one of the more successful playwrights of the period, asking for permission to dramatize her novel. She withheld her consent, explaining that if theaters began to show respectable, moral plays, young people of good Christian families would soon be permitted to see them and thus would develop the habit of regular theater-going, ultimately doing themselves more harm than good.

At the time, drama and book rights were obtained separately, and Mrs. Stowe made no attempt to secure the theatrical rights to her book. Another playwright, George L. Aiken, learned of her neglect, and wrote his own dramatization. It opened in New York early in the winter of 1853-54, and the public responded with the same fervor that it showed for the book. In order to meet the demand, the company gave three performances daily, always selling out, and the actors were so busy they remained in costume from noon until midnight, eating all of their meals backstage.

The dramatic version of *Uncle Tom's Cabin* was the most successful play ever produced in the American theater. At one time in the late 1850s, sixteen companies were playing it simultaneously in various parts of the United States. That record was eclipsed in 1868-72, when nineteen companies performed it. It was on the boards continuously somewhere in the United States from 1853 to 1934 without a single break.

Why Mrs. Stowe failed to protect the dramatic rights to *Uncle Tom's Cabin* is as puzzling as why she did not try to obtain some share of the royalties that Aiken earned. For under-standable reasons, she had refused to give permission to Hutchinson to dramatize the book, but then Aiken's work became a *fait accompli*. Not one word in her extant correspond-ence or in that of Professor Stowe indicates that either was aware of the existence of the most successful play of the era.

Aiken's version was also a resounding success in Great Britain, where it was played regularly until long after the beginning of the twentieth century. At least seventeen foreign-language versions of the play were shown in various countries; accurate statistics are unavailable, and the total may actually have been still larger. A musical version also enjoyed a resounding success in the United States and elsewhere in the English-speaking world for more than half a century, in spite of a pedestrian score and a dreadful libretto.

Mrs. Stowe's distinguished colleagues throughout the world, among them some of the greatest authors of the age, responded to *Uncle Tom's Cabin* with immediate enthusiasm and high praise. The generosity of American literary titans was unstinting.

Henry Wadsworth Longfellow wrote to the author, "It is one of the greatest triumphs recorded in literary history, to say nothing of the higher triumph of its moral effect." John Greenleaf Whittier declared, "What a glorious work Harriet Beecher Stowe has wrought!" James Russell Lowell not only admired the book but made it his immediate business to meet the author, and thereafter was her good friend.

Charles Dickens wrote to Mrs. Stowe, "I have read your book with the deepest interest and sympathy, and admire, more than I can express to you, both the generous feeling which inspired it, and the admirable power with which it is executed." Thomas Babbington Macaulay said the book was "the most valuable addition that America has made to English literature."

Heinrich Heine observed in all seriousness that Mrs. Stowe had written the greatest book since the Bible, which he was now studying again, thanks to her inspiration. His comment is said to have caused a run on Bibles in Paris bookstores. Leo Tolstoy later would link *Uncle Tom's Cabin* with *A Tale of Two Cities* and *Les Misérables* as examples of pure, moral art.

George Sand, who would call Mrs. Stowe a saint after they met, an encounter delayed by the New England lady's reluctance to have tea with a woman who openly took lovers, became rhapsodic over *Uncle Tom's Cabin*. She effectively silenced detractors when in the years immediately following the publication of the book it was called intellectual rubbish by some literary critics.

> If its judges, possessed with love of what they call "artistic work" find unskillful treatment in the book, look well at them to see if their eyes are dry.... Those who pretend...to judge...are often vanquished by their own feelings...when unwilling to avow them. This book is essentially domestic and of the family, this book, with its long discussions, its minute details, its portraits carefully studied. Mothers of families, young girls, little children, servants even, can read and understand them, and men themselves...cannot disdain them.

Henry James, writing about the period in *A Small Boy and Others*, treated Mrs. Stowe's work with the greatest respect.

> We lived and moved...with great intensity in Mrs. Stowe's novel.... There was, however, I think, for that triumphant work no classified condition; it was for no sort of reader, as distinct from any other sort, save indeed for Northern as differing from Southern; it knew the large felicity of gathering in alike the small and the simple and the big and the wise, and had above all the extraordinary fortune of finding itself for an immense number of people, much less a book than a state of vision, of feeling and of consciousness, in which they didn't sit and read and appraise and pass the time, but walked and talked and laughed and cried, and, in a manner of which Mrs. Stowe was the irresistible cause, generally conducted themselves.

The author of *Uncle Tom's Cabin*, world famous and solvent overnight, accepted the praise with astonishing calm. William Lloyd Garrison and antislavery members of the United States Senate and House of Representatives lauded her, and she thanked them, but did not misunderstand their motives. The leap from obscurity to renown made no change in her disposition. She was still a wife and mother, a human being struggling to establish within herself her relations with the Almighty. She was quietly pleased by the praise of other authors but neither felt nor displayed excessive pride.

The South reacted with violent hostility to *Uncle Tom's Cabin.* Several women wrote novels of their own describing the "true" conditions there, none of which was more than marginally successful.

In the months immediately following publication, Mrs. Stowe changed her habits only to the extent of visiting her publisher in Boston, spending a few days in Hartford with Mary and Isabella, then going to Brooklyn for a visit with the Henry Ward Beechers. There she learned that $1,200 was needed to buy the freedom of an escaped slave, and she immediately promised to raise the money, saying she would pay the entire sum herself if she failed. True to her word, she retraced her steps to Maine, pausing in Hartford and Boston, where she raised the better part of the sum, and then paid the difference out of her own pocket. This gesture was symbolic of a change in her life. Another was her new status as a celebrity. While visiting her brother in Brooklyn, she expressed a desire to attend a concert being given in Manhattan by the famous singer Jenny Lind. She was told that no tickets were available but stubbornly sent a letter to the management. Her name was recognized, and she was given two of the diva's own seats. After the performance, she was ushered backstage for a visit with Miss Lind, with whom she carried on a correspondence over the years.

During Mrs. Stowe's lifetime, a reaction to *Uncle Tom's Cabin* set in. It was no longer generally regarded as a literary masterpiece; on the contrary, many critics called it sentimental drivel, a work that had served useful purposes, rightly to be regarded as a literary curiosity only.

In more recent times that view has changed.

Carl Van Doren set the tone when he said that *Uncle Tom's Cabin* belongs to folklore. Others, among them such critics as Edmund Wilson, Charles H. Foster, and Van Wyck Brooks have gone much farther, not only decrying those who called the book "mere period trash" but praising it as literature of lasting stature.

Kenneth S. Lynn, in an introduction to a new edition of the book published by the Harvard University Press in 1962, declared, "Those critics who label *Uncle Tom's Cabin* good propaganda but bad art cannot have given sufficient time to the novel to meet its inhabitants. If they should ever linger over it long enough to take in the shrewdness, the energy, the truly Balzacian variousness of Mrs. Stowe's characterizations, they would surely cease to perpetuate one of the most unjust clichés in all of American criticism."

Edward Wagenknecht, in what he calls a "psychograph," *Harriet Beecher Stowe: The Known and the Unknown*, goes even farther. "Sometime in the 1930's I suggested to a distinguished publisher of limited editions that he bring out an *Uncle Tom's Cabin*. 'If you will do so,' I said, 'I will write you an introduction in which I will call it the greatest American novel.'" The edition was not published until many years later and contained an introduction by someone else, but the incident is typical of the swing of the pendulum. The book remains vital to an understanding of American history, but at present it is also being taught in courses on American literature at scores of universities. After a century and a quarter Mrs. Stowe has come into her own.

While Harriet Beecher Stowe was enjoying her first taste of life as a celebrity, traveling between Boston, New York, and Hartford, with stops in New Haven, Providence, and other cities, her husband's fortunes underwent a sudden change, too. Early in the summer of 1852, as the academic year at Lane Theological Seminary drew to a close, Calvin Stowe was able to free himself of his obligations there and planned to take his seat on the faculty at Bowdoin College, a post he had not yet filled. Much to his surprise, however, he was unexpectedly offered the chair in sacred literature at the Theological Seminary located in Andover, Massachusetts, a small town north of Boston, near the New Hampshire border.

It would be far more convenient for the Stowes to live there than in Maine, where snow made travel hazardous during the winter months; moreover, the Andover post paid an annual salary of $2,000, double what Professor Stowe would receive at Bowdoin. His wife's overnight success had removed financial pressures, but no one knew how long *Uncle Tom's Cabin* would continue to make money, and, in any event, he was the family's primary breadwinner. Mrs. Stowe rejoiced with him, and nothing in her correspondence indicates that she was currently earning almost as much in a week as he would be paid in a year.

With the appointment came the use of a house located on the Andover common that had been utilized in recent years as a gymnasium. Its refurbishing would have been beyond the family's means had it not been for Mrs. Stowe's windfall royalties. She took it upon herself to convert it into a home, and as the professor's departure from Cincinnati was delayed, she had to attend to the chores alone, squeezing the time into her busy schedule. Her obligations as a wife still took precedence over everything else, an attitude she would keep, however wealthy and famous she became. Her career was satisfying, but her duty was plain to her, and it took precedence.

The house was a rambling, three-story clapboard building painted white and had nine or ten chambers that could be used as bedrooms, making it ideal for a large family accustomed to putting up relatives and friends. Mrs. Stowe did not hesitate to use her own money making the place habitable, but lifelong frugality made her careful, and when the basic task was completed, at the end of October, 1852, she had confined her expenditures to approximately fifteen hundred dollars. Eight months earlier, that sum would have represented a small fortune, but now she was not concerned, nor was her husband. Neither realized it, but they had, in fact, rapidly adjusted to their new wealth and position.

Nevertheless, Southern critics who claimed that Mrs. Stowe was reveling in her new-found wealth were at best misinformed, at worst misled, by the propaganda that already portrayed her as a vicious, vulgar busybody. She bought no new clothes for herself, confined her furniture purchases to essentials, and celebrated only to the extent of having one new dress made for each of her daughters and one suit for each of her sons. New Englanders, particularly those like the Beechers who had been poor all of their lives, seldom indulged in ostentation. Henry Ward's Brooklyn congregation marveled because he still wore his old threadbare black suit, and his sister's admirers called attention to the simplicity of her appearance. Long after her death, Mrs. Stowe's children could not recall any period of her life when she had owned more than four or five dresses, or any occasion when she wore jewelry other than her wedding ring and a small brooch the professor had brought her from Europe soon after their marriage.

In her professional life, however, she did not shrink from taking full advantage of her new status. She happily accepted requests for articles from the *National Era* and *New York Independent,* and she deliberately began to gather material for future books. One, which she called "my Maine story," was far advanced. Glorifying the virtues of the rural people of the state, it would be called *The Pearl of Orr's Island,* but travel and the development of other projects would delay its completion and publication for a decade.

Her immediate concern was the adverse reaction to *Uncle Tom's Cabin* in the South. Still convinced that moderates and others of good will would rally to the antislavery cause once she had enlightened them, Mrs. Stowe failed to realize that her patronizing attitude had alienated virtually all Southerners. She had expected opposition only from the proslavery faction, and to their efforts she attributed the violent antagonism of the entire section of the country.

The vituperative mail she received from every part of the South disturbed her deeply. She claimed that she recognized the source of these attacks and consequently did not allow them to bother her, but in letter after letter she quoted from the more vitriolic, indicating that she was more upset than she was willing to admit. The reunited Stowe family settled into the new house, the professor began to teach at Andover, and his wife settled down in earnest to the preparation of a book of nonfiction, *A Key to Uncle Tom's Cabin,* which would be clear, concise, and, above all, factual, dealing with case histories that not only verified what she had written in her novel but demonstrated in detail even greater brutalities and more dismal conditions.

The abolitionists inundated her with material, but she refused to become the vehicle for their propaganda and rejected any story unsubstantiated by documentary proof. She was equally suspicious of data provided by such new acquaintances as Charles Sumner, United States senator from Massachusetts, one of the leaders of the antislavery forces in Congress. But she was less rigorous in demanding proof from an old friend and fellow member of the Semi-Colon Club, Senator Salmon P. Chase of Ohio.

The work was completed late in February, 1853, and Mrs. Stowe believed, when she handed it over to her Boston publisher, that it would have an impact greater than that of her novel. She did not yet know that literary lightning seldom strikes twice in the same place, but the *Key*, thanks to the storm created by its predecessor, nevertheless enjoyed an impressive success.

Published in May, 1853, during the author's absence from the country, it sold one hundred fifty thousand copies in the United States during its first year, subsequently enjoying a sale of an additional one hundred thousand copies. Sales in Great Britain, France, Germany, and ten other countries were modest but profitable.

If Mrs. Stowe did nothing else in writing the *Key* she demonstrated that she was a conscientious reporter. She marshaled her facts and allowed them to speak for themselves, disciplining her anger and avoiding flamboyance in her approach. *A Key to Uncle Tom's Cabin* created no great stir and possibly brought few new converts into the antislavery camp. At best, its influence was indirect, attracting readers unfamiliar with the novel to that work. But its effect on the author was profound. She was satisfied that she had overwhelmed her critics with facts they could not reasonably dispute, and those who continued to attack her must necessarily be proslavery fanatics, blind to the cruelty and injustice of the system they upheld. She was fond of quoting Kossuth: "No nation can remain free with whom freedom is a privilege and not a principle."

Declaring that "slavery is despotism," Mrs. Stowe devoted one section of the book to the many laws drawn and codified by the slave states to protect the institution. In clear, measured tones she enunciated her own position.

On which side, then, stands the American nation, in the great controversy which is now going on between self-government and despotism? On which side does America stand, in the great controversy for liberty of conscience?

Do foreign governments exclude their population from the reading of the Bible?—The slave of America is excluded by the most effectual means possible. Do we say, "Ah! but we read the Bible to our slaves, and present the gospel orally?"—This is precisely what religious despotism in Italy says. Do we say that we have no objection to our slaves reading the Bible, if they will stop there; but that with this there will come in a flood of general intelligence which will upset the existing state of things?—This is precisely what is said in Italy.

Do we say we should be willing that the slave read his Bible, but that he, in his ignorance, will draw false and erroneous conclusions from it, and for that reason we prefer to impart its truths to him orally?—This, also, is precisely what the religious despotism of Europe says.

Do we say, in our vain-glory, that despotic government dreads the coming in of anything calculated to elevate and educate the people?—And is there not the same dread through all the despotic slave governments in America?

On which side, then, does the American nation stand, in the great, last question of the age?

Some of her arguments were unanswerable. By its very nature, she said, slavery made even the most benevolent of its supporters callous. This denied the claim of the South that its public would not tolerate brutal excesses. Uncounted cruelties were performed, she maintained, because the people of the South were so inured to the system they no longer regarded these acts as cruel.

She also argued with telling effect that slave and free labor could not exist side by side in the same area. The mere existence of slavery corrupted the free laborer, robbing him of his dignity, destroying his incentives, filling him with shame, and making it impossible for him to work. Man should work not only for money but also because he takes pride in his accomplishments. The slave had neither motive, but as a free man he would work harder and produce more because he would share in the fruits of his labor.

In a final section of the *Key*, Mrs. Stowe returned to a favorite theme, and for the first time commanded a sufficiently large audience to make her voice heard. The churches of America, by which she meant the Protestant churches, were failing in their primary obligation to society by closing their eyes to slavery. If they stood together and took a firm stand, slavery in the United States would be destroyed overnight. They were ready enough to attack such minor dissipations as social dancing, but they were cowards when they claimed that slavery posed political and economic problems beyond their sphere of interest and jurisdiction. They mocked the meaning of Christianity when they declared, as the general assembly of the Presbyterian church had done in 1843, that it would be improper to take any position for or against slavery. The moral issue was paramount, and as all men were equal in the sight of God, any clergyman who refused to denounce slavery was actively supporting it.

The preparation of the *Key*, domestic obligations, an enlarged correspondence, and the writing of articles for the *New York Independent* and the *National Era* exhausted Mrs. Stowe. She was assuming too many burdens and was edging dangerously close to a condition that a later era would call nervous collapse. Her husband and children urged her to spare herself, but they remonstrated in vain. Before she was compelled to take to her bed, however, a kind, all-seeing Providence intervened on her behalf.

The Glasgow Anti-Slavery Society invited her to make a speaking tour of Scotland and England, offering to pay all of her expenses and those of Professor Stowe as well. She would be expected to address audiences in Edinburgh, Glasgow, Dundee, Aberdeen, Birmingham, and London. Mrs. Stowe had never spoken in public but, as daughter, wife, and sister of men who had spent their adult lives in pulpits and at lecterns, did not hesitate. She accepted the invitation, the professor obtained a short leave of absence, and it was arranged that the

Reverend Charles Beecher, who had just left his church but had not yet gone to another, would accompany them. The professor would spend about six weeks on the tour and then would return home. Mrs. Stowe, with her brother as her escort, would remain in London for several more weeks and thereafter would make a two- to three-month tour of France, Belgium, Switzerland, and some of the German states.

Mrs. Stowe bought a length of silk for a new dress but was too tired to stand for fittings. Her twin daughters, now sixteen, took care of packing her belongings for the journey and were careful to include the length of silk, suggesting that a dressmaker in London or Paris might be able to fashion the material for her.

In spite of her exhaustion, Mrs. Stowe was excited. Like so many Americans, she had long dreamed of going to Europe, and now she would follow in the footsteps of Benjamin Franklin and Thomas Jefferson, absorbing the culture of the Old World. She would visit the homes of Shakespeare and Milton, whose work she admired above all others. And in the spring, the season glorified by poets, she would travel through the English countryside.

The result of the journey was a new book, prepared by Professor Stowe and the Reverend Charles Beecher as well as Mrs. Stowe. Entitled *Sunny Memories of Foreign Lands,* it was published in 1854 and, because it bore the magical name of Harriet Beecher Stowe, it sold more than fifty thousand copies in the United States. A London edition, brought out the following year, sold equally well in Great Britain and its colonies. Mrs. Stowe's contribution consisted of letters she wrote on the journey, principally to her children and various relatives. These were edited, and most personal references to family matters were deleted. Read in conjunction with Charles Beecher's journal, they give a detailed day-by-day account of a nineteenth-century American pilgrim's progress.

The portion written by Professor Stowe challenges the modern reader and could have been of interest to only a few of his contemporaries. Many American newspapers, including the moderate press of the North, had been critical of the journey, claiming with considerable justice that Harriet Beecher Stowe intended to capitalize on her recent fame by winning converts abroad to the antislavery cause.

The professor's position was delicate. For many years he had preached the cause of gradual emancipation, but his wife was being hailed as the great champion of the antislavery forces, so he felt compelled to take a firmer stand himself. He wrote an introduction to *Sunny Memories*, fifty-four pages of very small print, which began with a long, apologetic diatribe in which he attacked slavery as "a blight, a canker, a poison, in the very heart of our republic." Having established his new position to his own satisfaction, he gave exhaustively detailed accounts of the thirteen meetings he addressed on his wife's behalf when she proved too shy to do so. These reports are dry and detached and include data on the business conducted at each meeting. They could have been prepared as minutes by the secretaries of the various antislavery organizations involved, and the omission of the introduction in no way would detract from Mrs. Stowe's story, which combines an account of the Cinderella-like triumphal tour of a recently unknown housewife with a travel guide written by a wide-eyed tourist.

Professor Stowe has been accused, with some justice, of thrusting himself into the limelight at his wife's expense. In all fairness to him, however, his position as the husband of a celebrity was difficult, and he had not yet grown accustomed to it. Many years would pass before he developed poise and accepted his position with a sense of humor, as he did when he told a gate-crasher, who informed him she would rather see Mrs. Stowe, "I entirely agree with you, madam."

Harriet Beecher Stowe, her husband, and her brother left New York late in March, 1853, and two and a half weeks later they arrived in Liverpool. They sailed on one of the new clipper ships, vessels that were the wonder of the maritime world and pride of the American merchant marine, so named because they clipped all previous speed records. Indeed, seasoned travelers claimed the clippers sacrificed comfort for speed. Sleeping quarters were cramped, public rooms were small, and deck space was inadequate; even worse, the clippers, according to many, pitched and rolled heavily, even in calm weather. Mrs. Stowe, whose sea ventures had been confined to river packets, lake paddlewheelers, and occasional rowboats to small islands off the Maine coast, was certain she would be miserable and carried in her hand luggage a variety of patent medicines guaranteed to cure seasickness. To her surprise, she enjoyed the voyage enormously, discovering for herself, as have countless other travelers, that the sea is invigorating. She took long walks around the open deck, fascinated equally by the billowing sails and the changing moods of the ocean. She slept well, ate heartily, and at meals bombarded the captain and his mates with questions about navigation, the relative merits of various types of ships, and the schooling of seamen. As the days passed, her fatigue lessened, and by the time the ship landed at Liverpool on April 11, 1853, her health had been restored On the eve of her forty-second birthday, she was ready for the first real holiday-adventure of her life.

If two volumes of her letters offer any indication of her true feelings during her sojourn abroad, Mrs. Stowe's mood was as cheerful as the title of her book suggests. Unlike her husband, who seemed obsessed by the slavery question, she virtually confined her discussion of the subject to British newspaper clippings on the thirteen meetings she attended. Scenery for its own sake still failed to impress her, except in isolated instances. She was interested almost exclusively in people—past and present—and their living conditions.

She learned a great deal about the great Queen Elizabeth, whom she had admired as a child but now found "repulsive and disagreeable." She was equally harsh in her opinion of unenlightened contemporary monarchs and called Napoleon III, who had just seized the throne of France in a coup, a "tyrant."

The Scots drank to excess. She was alarmed by the number of squalid gin shops she saw in the slums of London, Liverpool, and Birmingham. The smoke and soot of the industrial Midlands created an atmosphere that destroyed the morals and spirits of the poor. "I know of no one circumstance more unfavorable to moral purity than the necessity of being physically dirty." She saw dirt everywhere, including Notre Dame Cathedral, and everywhere it depressed her. Americans, she concluded, were cleaner than the British and the Continentals.

Chauvinism occasionally hampered her reportorial objectivity, and prejudices sometimes made her myopic, too. Sundays were pleasant in Catholic countries, she felt, but the atmosphere was not conducive to political liberty. "There is not a single nation, possessed of a popular form of government, which has not our Puritan theory of the Sabbath—Protestant Switzerland, England, Scotland, and America." Furthermore, true freedom required that the individual discipline himself, a habit best acquired on the Puritan Sabbath.

In spite of her occasional criticisms, Mrs. Stowe enjoyed herself thoroughly. She was thrilled by old Roman walls, the ruins of castles, and crumbling monasteries, even though her hosts were amused by her enthusiasm. She was impressed by the exquisite manners of the upper-class English. She was awed by the masterpieces she saw in galleries and churches.

Although Mrs. Stowe had dabbled in painting and had taught art to young girls, she was aware of her own limitations in the field. She had made no serious study of painting or sculpture and, until now, had thought of architecture as the trees of New England, which she could describe in minute detail.

She discovered the Gothic style on this trip to Europe, and promptly fell in love with it. At no time was her reaction to architecture or other art forms intellectual: Either she felt or did not, and, more often than not, religion found a place in her feeling. "In this Gothic architecture," she wrote, "we see earnest northern races, whose nature was a composite of influences from pine forest, mountain, and storm, expressing, in vast proportions and gigantic masonry, those ideas of infinite duration and existence which Christianity opened before them. A barbaric wildness mingles itself with fanciful, ornate abundance; it is the blossoming of northern forests." The Houses of Parliament were perfect examples of what she regarded as pure Gothic architecture.

She decided there was a strong Gothic quality in Shakespeare, who created "an ideal world of men and women." She was overwhelmed by the painting of Rubens, although she found it difficult to admire his abundantly lush nudes, and she insisted he was like Shakespeare, although she did not explain the similarity. By the same token, Rembrandt resembled Hawthorne, and the architect who had designed Melrose Abbey was a Mozart among architects.

Mrs. Stowe could be stubborn in her likes and dislikes. She knew that St. Paul's Cathedral, London's old metropolitan church, which was completely rebuilt after the Great Fire of

1666, was universally regarded as an architectural gem, but it failed to impress her. When asked her reasons, she could only shrug and reply, "When I look at it, I don't *feel* anything."

She was better able to articulate her reaction to the paintings of Rubens: "Rubens, the great, joyous, full-souled, all-powerful Rubens!—there he was, full as ever of triumphant, abounding life; disgusting and pleasing; making me laugh and making me angry; defying me to dislike him; dragging me at his chariot wheels; in despite of my protests forcing me to confess that there was no other but he."

Her admiration for Rubens did not adequately prepare her for his great *Descent from the Cross* in Antwerp Cathedral, and it stunned her.

> My first sensation was of astonishment, blank, absolute, overwhelming. After all that I had seen, I had no idea of a painting like this. I was lifted off my feet, as much as by Cologne Cathedral, or Niagara Falls, so that I could neither reason nor think whether I was pleased or not. It is difficult, even now, to analyze the sources of this wonderful power. The excellence of this picture does not lie, like Raphael's, in a certain ideal spirituality, by which the scene is raised above earth to a heavenly sphere; but rather in a power, strong, human, almost homely, by which, not an ideal, but the real scene is forced home upon the heart.

Mrs. Stowe could find nothing good to say about the theater and in both London and Paris refused invitations to attend performances of currently popular plays. At no time either before or after her trip to England did she deign to explain her hatred for the medium in which Shakespeare's work was still being played. She was logical when logic best suited her purposes, but when it failed to accomplish that end she clung stubbornly to her prejudices. Throughout her life, Mrs. Stowe agreed with Henry Ward Beecher that the theater was "a painted harlot," but that did not prevent her from quoting at length from the plays of Shakespeare and hailing them as "words so pure that only Divine Providence could have inspired them." She was still a Beecher, and consequently abided by her own rules.

Her pleasure in her first trip abroad became greater when she found it was unnecessary for her to speak in public. Professor Stowe, long accustomed to the lectern, happily accepted the chore, and it was enough for his celebrated wife to be seen, to shake hands, and to exchange a few pleasantries with those who wanted to meet her.

Wherever she went in Scotland and England, huge throngs gathered, sometimes watching her in silence, sometimes breaking into spontaneous cheers. It was startling to her to be greeted everywhere as a celebrity, to be treated with deference, and she could not accustom herself to it. Yet, one suspects that she, perhaps unconsciously, liked being treated as a famous person, once she recovered from her initial bewilderment. In all, she spent approximately five months abroad, two months in Great Britain and the rest on the Continent, yet 70 percent of *Sunny Memories* is devoted to her time in Scotland and England, where she was a celebrity (on the Continent she avoided recognition whenever she could and became a simple tourist).

Yet only because she felt secure within herself can she have been able to withstand the ordeal to which she was subjected in Scotland and England. Great lords and ladies were presented to her and cherished the introduction. The greatest authors of the age accepted her without cavil as an equal. Statesmen and politicians who made daily headlines in the press of the world bowed over her hand and drank tea with her. Poor farmers, miners, and industrial workers stood patiently for hours, waiting for a glimpse of her as she passed.

She received more gifts than she could enumerate, for both herself and the antislavery movement. The people of Scotland presented her with a thousand gold sovereigns for the cause on a handsome silver platter as a personal gift. The Friends of Aberdeen filled a lovely gold-embroidered purse with gold, giving her the purse and donating the money to the movement. The people of Ireland lined a wooden box with gold, stuffed it with gold coins to be used as she saw fit to aid the cause, and presented it to her. Gifts from individuals, equally impressive, included a bracelet of gold shaped like a slave's shackle from the Duchess of Sutherland; a pen of solid gold, to be used to write new antislavery tracts, from a group of English school children; and a silver inkstand, presented by the ladies of Surrey Chapel, which featured a figure representing Religion giving freedom to a slave.

Mrs. Stowe's favorite present, which she did not receive until her return to the United States, was a testimonial inspired and arranged for by Lord Shaftesbury. A total of 562,448 women throughout the British Empire affixed their names to a document called "An Affectionate and Christian Address from the Women of Great Britain to the Women of America." Their signatures filled twenty-six leather-bound volumes, each embossed in gold with the American eagle. This expression of solidarity with the antislavery cause became one of Mrs. Stowe's most treasured possessions.

Occasionally the excitement overwhelmed her: At one point, a crowd estimated by the press at somewhere between five and ten thousand people gathered outside Glasgow Cathedral to cheer her, and she became so shy that the strain sent her to bed for a day. She suffered similarly three or four other times, but, in general, she remained in good health and maintained a grueling schedule of public appearances, sightseeing, and socializing with prominent Britons.

In Great Britain, the modest lady who invariably wore a straw bonnet and a dull cape of gray wool had no enemies, only admirers who could find no fault in her. Only now did she begin to realize the full effect that *Uncle Tom's Cabin* had on others, but she still felt she deserved no tributes. She told George Richmond, the most famous portrait painter of the day, for whom she reluctantly sat, "If people really knew me they wouldn't make such a fuss over me." There seems to have been little likelihood that adulation would turn her head.

In Liverpool the Stowes and Charles Beecher were the guests of Mrs. Edward Cropper, daughter of Lord Chief Justice Denman, who was active in the antislavery movement. Others who worked for the cause and were also prominent in the

League for Temperance were their hosts in Scotland, and in Birmingham they stayed with Joseph Sturge, a Quaker who led an Empire-wide campaign to boycott slave-grown cotton. In London, where the visitors spent the better part of their sojourn in Great Britain, they were so much in demand that they stayed for a time with one Congregational clergyman, then with another. They were usually entertained by people active in the antislavery movement, among them the Earl of Carlisle, who had written an introduction to an English edition of *Uncle Tom's Cabin,* and his sister, the Duchess of Sutherland.

On two occasions, the Archbishop of Canterbury sat beside her at dinner and was impressed by her grasp of theology as well as her ability to quote long passages from the Bible. Dickens, Thackeray, and Macaulay accepted her as a peer and talked shop with her. In her relations with them, she wrote to her children, she soon lost her feeling of awe and was completely at her ease. She was surprised, then encouraged, when she discovered their writing problems were similar to her own.

She charmed the Prime Minister, Lord John Russell. The Earl of Shaftesbury, the Duke of Argyll, and Sir Charles Trevelyan were among her most ardent admirers. She also became friendly with two future prime ministers: Lord Palmerston, Home Secretary and former Foreign Secretary, and William Gladstone, Chancellor of the Exchequer. The former called her a "marvelously sensible lady." Gladstone, destined to become the greatest British statesman of the century, observed that although she knew little of world affairs, Mrs. Stowe could have become successful in politics, had she been a man, because she "instinctively grasped the essentials of issues."

Scores of others from Britain's ruling class met and conversed with Mrs. Stowe at dinners, luncheons, and teas. She was thrilled when she first encountered Lady Byron and was overjoyed when the great poet's widow remarked that her husband would have approved of *Uncle Tom's Cabin.* The two women became increasingly intimate, and on several occasions had tea together in private.

The visitors attended many religious services, of course, and Mrs. Stowe was pleasantly surprised to realize that Anglican thought was not so alien to Congregationalism and Presbyterianism as she had always assumed. But "the intoning at St. Paul's has an unpleasing, nasal quality," she declared, dismissing the most renowned choir in the Anglo-Saxon world.

English sermons, she wrote, "do not recognize the existence ... of inquiry or doubt in the popular mind," but "in American sermons there is always more or less time employed in explaining, proving, and answering objections to, the truths enforced." English sermons made a deep impression on her, and she wrote to her father that they were "fervent, affectionate, and evangelical in spirit," usually delivered on "topics of practical benevolence." In fact, she told him, "The aspect of the religious mind of England is very encouraging in this respect; that it is humble, active, and practical. Churchman, Puseyite, Dissenter, Presbyterian, Independent, Quaker ... I have found among them all evidence of that true piety which consists in a humble and childlike spirit of obedience to God, and a sincere desire to do good to men."

Mrs. Stowe's sense of humor did not desert her and helped her to keep a sense of balance in spite of her busy schedule. In one letter to her children she wrote:

> The general topic of remark on meeting me seems to be, that I am not so bad-looking as they were afraid I was; and I do assure you that when I have seen the things that are put up in the shop windows here with my name under them, I have been in wondering admiration at the boundless loving-kindness of my English and Scottish friends in keeping up such a warm heart for such a Gorgon. I should think that the Sphinx in the London Museum might have sat for most of them. I am going to make a collection of these portraits to bring home to you. There is a great variety of them, and they will be useful,

like the Irishman's guide-board, which showed where the road did not go.

That she went about her sightseeing in the same spirit is indicated by a passage in a letter to her sister Mary.

I can compare the embarrassment of our London life, with its multiplied solicitations and infinite stimulants to curiosity and desire, only to that annual perplexity which used to beset us in our childhood on Thanksgiving Day. Like Miss Edgeworth's philosophic little Frank, we are obliged to make out a list of what man *must* want, and of what he *may* want; and in our list of the former we set down, in large and decisive characters, one quiet day for the exploration and enjoyment of Windsor.

The ride was done all too soon. About eleven o'clock we found ourselves going up the old stone steps to the castle. We went first through the state apartments. The principal thing that interested me was the ball-room, which was a perfect gallery of Vandyke's paintings. After leaving the ball-room we filed off to the proper quarter to show our orders for the private rooms. The state apartments, which we had been looking at, are open at all times, but the private apartments can only be seen in the Queen's absence, and by a special permission, which had been procured for us on that occasion by the kindness of the Duchess of Sutherland.

One of the first objects that attracted my attention upon entering the vestibule was a baby's wicker wagon, standing in one corner. It was much such a carriage as all mothers are familiar with; such as figures largely in the history of almost every family. . . .

We were bent upon looking up the church which gave rise to Gray's "Elegy in a Country Churchyard," intending when we got there to have a little scene over it; Mr. S., in all the conscious importance of having been there before, assuring us that he knew exactly where it was. So, after some difficulty with our coachman, and being stopped at one church which would not answer our purpose in any respect, we were at last set down by one which looked authentic; embowered in mossy elms, with a most ancient and goblin yew-tree, an ivory-mantled tower, all perfect as could be. Here, leaning on the old fence, we repeated the Elegy, which certainly applies here as beautifully as language could apply.

Imagine our chagrin, on returning to London, at being informed that we had not been to the genuine churchyard after all. The gentleman who wept over the scenes of his early days on the wrong doorstep was not more grievously disappointed. However, he and we could both console ourselves with the reflection that the emotion was admirable, and wanted only the right place to make it the most appropriate in the world.

Sometimes Mrs. Stowe's ignorance of local customs created embarrassments for her, but she took these in her stride with the aplomb of the seasoned traveler.

I have been quite amused with something which has happened lately. This week the "Times" has informed the United Kingdom that Mrs. Stowe is getting a new dress made! It wants to know if Mrs. Stowe is aware what sort of a place her dress is being made in; and there is a letter from a dressmaker's apprentice stating that it is being made up piecemeal, in the most shockingly distressed dens of London, by poor, miserable white slaves, worse treated than the plantation slaves of America!

Now Mrs. Stowe did not know anything of this, but simply gave the silk into the hands of a friend, and was in due time waited on in her own apartment by a very respectable-appearing woman, who offered to make the dress, and lo! this is the result! Since the publication of this piece I have received earnest missives, from various parts of the country, begging me to interfere, hoping that I was not going to patronize the white slavery of England, and that I would employ my talents equally against oppression in every form. Could these people only know in what sweet simplicity I had been living in the State of Maine, where the only dressmaker of our circle was an intelligent, refined, well-educated woman who was considered as the equal of us all, and whose spring and fall ministrations to our wardrobes was regarded a double pleasure,—a friendly visit as well as a domestic assistance, —I say, could they know all this, they would see how guiltless I was in the matter. I verily never thought but that the nice, pleasant person who came to measure me for my silk dress was going to take it home and make it herself; it never occurred to me that she was the head of an establishment.

Mrs. Stowe's lack of worldliness found expression in many ways. "I am always finding out, a day or two after, that I have been with somebody very remarkable, and did not know it at the time," she wrote. "One has a strange mythological feeling about the existence of people of whom one hears for many years without ever seeing them."

The tidbits of information she drops are as fascinating as her more penetrating observations. William Makepeace Thackeray, almost precisely her own age and regarded by most contemporaries as Dickens's only serious rival, "at first glance more nearly resembles a clergyman than a writer of novels, but he, in his conversation, is so merry, so full of wit and so clever in his understanding of human nature that his true vocation soon reveals itself." Dickens looked far younger than she had anticipated, and was simultaneously polite and cheerful.

Her own rigid standards notwithstanding, Mrs. Stowe was becoming more tolerant. English ladies, regardless of their age, wore low-cut evening gowns that she privately found shocking. She could excuse them, however, because they kept their youthful figures and complexions, thanks to physical exercise and abstention from the performance of household chores, which were the province of superbly trained servants who took pride in their work. There is a wistful note in her references to English servants.

One of the secrets of Mrs. Stowe's success in England was her refusal to put on airs, to be anything but herself. On one occasion, she enlivened a dinner-table discussion of fox hunting, which she privately regarded as a cruel sport, by relating that hunting was a serious business on the American frontier, where the men of a family were forced to hunt if they wanted to eat meat. She also told a story, probably made up on

the spot, about an Ohio backwoodsman who snuffed out his
bedside candle with a rifle shot.

The elegance of aristocratic English homes and the comfort of middle-class dwellings unfailingly impressed her, and
she lovingly described damask wallpapers, velvet chair cover-
ings, and silver tea services in letters to her sisters and
daughters. Even when enjoying herself, she could not help
thinking in larger terms, as an author. "A man builds a house
in England with the expectation of living in it and leaving it to
his children; while we shed our houses in America as easily as a
snail does his shell."

On the last day of May, after seeing Professor Stowe off for
America, laden with a valise crammed with presents for the
children, Mrs. Stowe and her brother departed from England
for the Continent. Her taste of high life among the great had
been pleasant, but now she longed for the quiet that only
anonymity could secure. Wherever and whenever possible, she
decided, she would not reveal her identity.

She and Charles Beecher traveled by easy stages, and on
June 3 they reached Paris. Like Benjamin Franklin, Thomas
Jefferson, Thomas Paine, and Washington Irving before her,
and like millions of Americans who came after her, Harriet
Beecher Stowe was dazzled by the City of Light. In less than
twenty-four hours she fell in love with it.

> I have been out all the morning exploring shops, streets,
> boulevards, and seeing and hearing life in Paris. When
> one has a pleasant home and friends to return to, this gay,
> bustling, vivacious, graceful city is one of the most
> charming things in the world. . . .
> I wish the children could see these Tuileries with
> their statues and fountains, men, women and children
> seated in family groups under the trees, chatting, reading
> aloud, working muslin,—children driving hoop, playing
> ball, all alive and chattering French. Such fresh, pretty
> girls as are in the shops here! *Je suis ravé,* as they say. In
> short I am decidedly in a French humor, and am taking
> things quite *couleur de rose.*

For several days, Mrs. Stowe played the role of the sightseer to the hilt. She walked along the Seine, gaped at the gargoyles of Notre Dame Cathedral, felt wicked when she ate cheese in a Montmartre artists' restaurant, and walked through art galleries until her feet felt as though they would drop from her legs. At the Louvre, she discovered Rembrandt and at first was awed, then tried to analyze her feelings more closely, writing that in the work of this great artist she found "if not a commanding, a drawing influence, a full satisfaction for one part of my nature...a somber richness and mysterious gloom...appealing, because our life is a haunted one; the simplest thing is a mystery; the invisible world always lies round us like a shadow."

Paris was "a lotos-eater's paradise. I am released from care; I am unknown, unknowing." To an extent, Mrs. Stowe was deceiving herself. Her hostess in Paris, a woman she describes only as "Mrs. C.," an American expatriate, was well aware of her identity, and at two dinner parties *Uncle Tom's Cabin* was a principal subject of discussion. But these were quiet affairs, and most of the other guests were fellow Americans.

She was taken to restaurants frequented by French writers, but in her correspondence she mentions only two. One was Victor Hugo, living in self-imposed exile in protest against the tyranny of Napoleon III. The other was George Sand, who had written with such nobility and generosity about *Uncle Tom's Cabin*. Mrs. Stowe hoped to see and meet her and was stunned when she was told that respectable people did not receive Mme. Sand, who not only lived openly with her lovers but had ruined the lives of two young men—Alfred de Musset, the poet, and Chopin, the composer. Not until the American felt more sure of herself would such a meeting take place.

During her one-week sojourn in Paris, Mrs. Stowe's portrait was painted by a distinguished artist, Belloc, director of the Imperial School of Design, whose wife had been the French translator of *Uncle Tom's Cabin*. She also attended the literary salon of Lady Elgin, where she met several poets she did not identify in her correspondence. But after she left Paris, her incognito was relatively complete. There were no dinner parties, no meetings with the great and near great, no anti-slavery rallies to attend. In Lyons the pleasures of the table overwhelmed her and she was afraid she was putting on weight. In Antwerp she fell in love with Rubens. The Alps left her breathless, and she described their beauty with a rapture she seldom expressed for nature for its own sake. At the Castle of Chillon, she inscribed her name on a pillar beneath that of Byron and, because of her friendship with his widow, felt close to him.

Occasionally, to be sure, the idyll was flawed. Tobacco smoke in the saloon of a Rhine steamer gave her a headache, making it impossible for her to enjoy the beauties of Heidelberg. The rarified air of the higher Alpine passes made it difficult for her to breathe, and she was afraid she might faint. But these brief periods of unpleasantness were exceptional.

In a number of German cities, she searched for places where Martin Luther had lived, preached, and taught. Because of her husband's enthusiasm for the works of Goethe she did the same in memory of the latter, but her correspondence hints that she was herself familiar only with his *Diary*. That was all of his work that she had wanted to read because she regarded him as "too egotistical."

She and Charles Beecher wandered on Alpine trails by the hour, her fatigue forgotten, much as they had walked through the Connecticut woods as children. Here in Switzerland, she enjoyed a carefree holiday, which she celebrated by painting mountain flowers and mountain scenes in watercolors. She recognized her efforts as crude and amateurish, but she did not care. She would take the paintings to her children and sought no other audience for them.

Charles was the perfect companion for such a journey, for Mrs. Stowe could relax more completely in his company than with any other Beecher, even Henry Ward. Their tastes were similar, although Charles was more partial to music and less interested in literature, but they were equally fascinated by great painting.

On occasion, too, Charles could forget he was a Presbyterian clergyman, as his sister could that she came from a family of ministers. One night they dined under the stars at the

Jardin Mabille on the Champs-Elysées in Paris, and Mrs. Stowe discovered with alarm there were music and dancing there. But later she watched waltzing couples with pleasure, assured by her brother that dancing was not really a sin, and "almost" wished she herself could waltz! The daughter of Lyman Beecher and wife of Calvin Stowe was receiving a liberal education.

Never in her adult life had she enjoyed such good health. No work kept her at a desk; she was free of financial worries and had no immediate anxiety for the welfare of her husband and children. "One would almost think her incapable of fatigue," her brother wrote from Switzerland after she had spent a long day hiking and scrambling over rocks near the timber line. The absence of responsibility was a new experience, and she relished it, sometimes wishing she could prolong her holiday.

Occasionally Mrs. Stowe's shield of anonymity was penetrated. Other guests at her Geneva hotel discovered her identity and thronged about her, telling her how much they had liked *Uncle Tom's Cabin,* and the same thing happened in several other places. At such times, Mrs. Stowe was gracious and patient, willingly discussing her book with fellow tourists. Her success was still new to her, and Charles Beecher hinted that she liked being recognized so far from home.

Trying to crowd as much sightseeing as possible into a short period, sister and brother maintained a pace that would have exhausted most travelers. They seldom spent more than a night or two in any place, and everywhere visited churches, museums, and spots of scenic and historical interest. Mrs. Stowe also learned to linger in restaurants and cafés where she could observe people, and often found herself devising stories about strangers. But it did not later occur to her to develop foreign backgrounds for any of her fiction. She was a stranger in Europe, tentatively groping toward an understanding of foreign people and their customs. No matter how romantic and sentimental her approach, she clung to the principle that she could and should write only about worlds she knew.

Mrs. Stowe was not yet aware of the extent to which travel was expanding her outlook. Her point of view remained parochial, but observing how others lived was beginning to influence her, and she peered for the first time over the high, inflexible walls of Protestantism that hemmed her in. Other journeys would have to be made before she lowered those walls.

After spending three months on the Continent, Mrs. Stowe and the Reverend Charles Beecher retraced their steps to Paris, where they stayed for a few days, and then returned to England. Again she was overwhelmed by friends and admirers, and was tempted to remain for an additional month or six weeks. But her conscience asserted itself, reminding her that duties to her family and work awaited her.

Stifling regrets, Mrs. Stowe booked passage for New York on a steamer, the *Arctic,* early in September, 1853. Having already traveled eastward on a clipper ship, she decided to try another mode of transportation on the homeward journey. Her adventure would not end until she walked into the Andover house and resumed her responsibilities.

10

Refreshed by her long holiday, Harriet Beecher Stowe threw herself into her work with unprecedented vigor in the autumn of 1853, the supposedly frail state of her constitution forgotten. Her children were her first consideration, and she gave them her full attention, scheduling other activities at hours when they did not need her. Her critics in the South accused her of neglecting her duties as a mother, but these charges were false. The demands on her time multiplied as her fame continued to grow, but she never faltered in the discharge of her maternal obligations. Her family still came first, and everthing else had to be crowded into spare time.

The home life of the Stowe family was not what it had been prior to the publication of *Uncle Tom's Cabin*. A full-time cook was now in charge of the kitchen, a maid took care of the cleaning and other chores, and a woman who came to the house two days each week did the laundry and mending, which Mrs. Stowe had always loathed. The rewards of financial security were obvious, and the Stowe children were very much aware of their mother's success.

Professor Stowe's reactions to this are difficult to fathom. His wife's royalties supported the family's vastly increased living expenses, her mail came to the house each day in a special sack, and her growing social circle included prominent persons in many fields. Attempts have been made to show that Calvin Stowe sulked, that he was jealous of his wife's success, but no proof has ever been offered. Indeed, the contrary appears to have been the case. Like most men of the mid-nineteenth century, he remained very much the head of his family, and his wife made no move in business without seeking his advice and obtaining his assent, even though he found it difficult to grasp even the basic essentials of finance. What kept the marriage harmonious was Mrs. Stowe's genuine awe of her husband's intellect. He was one of America's leading experts in Biblical history, he read voraciously and remembered everything he read, and he was at ease with even the most distinguished vistors, able to discuss any subject with them.

Consequently Mrs. Stowe deferred to him in all matters of the mind, and her high regard for him was not simulated. Thus domestic tranquility was preserved, even though she was now the primary breadwinner and her reputation became far greater than his. Occasionally, in their correspondence, she complained briefly of his physical laziness, which increased as the years passed. But this appears to have been a minor irritation that did not influence their relationship to any marked degree.

As loyal to his wife as she was to him, Professor Stowe never openly spoke or wrote resentfully of her success. There can be little doubt, however, that he felt some frustrations. Slender until the 1850s, he began to put on weight soon after the publication of *Uncle Tom's Cabin*, and throughout the rest of his long life he became increasingly obese, ultimately finding it an effort to haul himself out of a chair. But there is no indication in the couple's correspondence or elsewhere that either recognized the cause of his deteriorating physical condition.

As soon as Mrs. Stowe returned from Europe, she actively re-entered the struggle to abolish slavery. Still too shy to accept any of the hundreds of speaking engagements offered to her, she contributed her services in the way she knew best, writing speeches for others to deliver. She refused to accept fees or public credit for such activities.

Immediate arrangements were made for the publication of *Sunny Memories* with the firm of Phillips and Sampson, the successors to the John P. Jewett Company; her London publishers, Sampson, Low and Company, happily accepted the book for publication there. The demand for her work was so great that she purchased the plates of her 1843 collection of short stories, *The Mayflower,* from the Harper brothers and, after revising and editing a number of stories, gave the book to Phillips and Sampson for publication in 1855. It was a great success in both the United States and Great Britain, reaching a readership eager to buy anything from her pen.

In the final months of 1853 and throughout 1854, she wrote an average of one magazine article every two weeks. All were attacks on slavery, and, although she introduced no new arguments into the controversy, the public was given no chance to forget where she stood. The slavery issue was intensified by the struggle in Congress to allow or prohibit the extension of the institution to the Nebraska and Kansas territories, and Mrs. Stowe needed no urging to do her part. She wrote "An Appeal to the Women of America," which she had printed in pamphlet form at her own expense. It was widely quoted in the Northern press, and tens of thousands of copies were distributed free of charge.

The Stowe house must have been crowded in the autumn and early winter of 1853. It was becoming a rallying center for antislavery activities, and among the vistors to Andover in the autumn were William Lloyd Garrison, with whom Mrs. Stowe maintained a long correspondence, never completely accepting his advocacy of immediate abolition, and Frederick Douglass. Charles Beecher prolonged a visit so that he could edit the galley proofs of *Sunny Memories,* and was followed by his father and stepmother. Lyman Beecher, now seventy-eight years of age, was living in retirement in Boston and came to Andover for a specific purpose. His memory was beginning to fail, as he himself realized, so at Mrs. Stowe's suggestion he spent his days before her parlor fire, dictating his memoirs to Charles.

Her own energy still inexhaustible, Mrs. Stowe arranged a Boston lecture series on slavery, the speakers to include her husband, Horace Greeley, and Wendell Phillips, the orator and reformer, among others. She also brought out a new edition of her first book, the geography she had written with her sister Catherine, now the founder of the American Woman's Educational Association, an organization active in establishing schools for girls throughout the Middle West. At first glance, the reissue of the geography seems a strange project, but Mrs. Stowe had her reasons: She injected new material into it, unequivocal antislavery propaganda.

Her correspondence with others in the movement, in Great Britain as well as in the United States, was exceptionally energetic during this year. She spared no effort in her letters, which frequently ran as long as three thousand words. Afraid that his sister was recklessly expending her energies, the Reverend Henry Ward Beecher urged her to hire a secretary to whom she could dictate her letters, speeches, and articles. Others in the family were also concerned. Her sister Mary Perkins joined in the campaign from Hartford, and the Reverend Edward Beecher wrote to her from Boston. But Mrs. Stowe refused to give the idea serious consideration. Longfellow had no secretary, she replied, nor did Whittier. The last thing she wanted was to be regarded as ostentatious by fellow authors. By utilizing her time with care she would manage alone.

It was an unfailing source of satisfaction to her that no one in the South had written an effective reply to the *Key to Uncle Tom's Cabin*. What she failed to realize was that most critics in the South now placed her with Garrison and other fanatics and felt it would be a waste of their time to engage in debate with her.

For, despite her increased activity on behalf of the antislavery movement, she still thought of herself as a moderate.

Late in 1853, in a contribution to a booklet called "Uncle Sam's Emancipation," she wrote:

> The great error of controversy is, that it is ever ready to assail *persons* rather than *principles*. The slave system as a *system*, perhaps concentrates more wrong than any other now existing, and yet those who live under and in it may be as we see, enlightened, generous, and amenable to reason. If the system alone is attacked, such minds will be the first to perceive its evils, and to turn against it; but if the system be attacked through individuals, self-love, wounded pride, and a thousand natural feelings, will be at once enlisted for its preservation.

In a letter written at about the same time to Daniel R. Goodloe, a Southern intellectual, Mrs. Stowe spoke of her goal with even greater candor.

> It has been my earnest desire to address myself to southern minds, for I have always believed that there was slumbering at the South, energy enough to reform its evils, could it only be aroused.
>
> It has seemed to me that many who have attacked the system, have not understood the southern character, nor appreciated what is really good in it. I think *I* have, at least I have tried, during this whole investigation, to balance my mind by keeping before it the most agreeable patterns of southern life and character....
>
> It seems to me that truly noble minds ought to consider *that* the best friendship which refuses to defend their faults, but rather treats them as excrescences which ought to be severed, and what is true of individuals is true of countries.
>
> I respect and admire the true chivalric, noble ideal of the southern man, and therefore more indignantly reprobate all that which is no part of him, being the result of an unnatural institution, and which is unworthy of him, and therein, I think, show myself more fully a friend than those who undertake to defend faults and all.

It was becoming increasingly difficult for Mrs. Stowe to practice what she preached. Elements of moderation are discernible in *Uncle Tom's Cabin,* although few in the South could find them. The *Key* is a far harsher document because she was replying to critics who had attacked her integrity. Soon, convinced that the time had come to do another anti-slavery novel that would further the cause of emancipation, she displayed still less charity toward her foes.

Mrs. Stowe did not settle down to the writing of her new book until 1855, by which time the dispute over slavery was reaching alarming proportions. A mini-war was being waged in Kansas, with both North and South sending in volunteers who would help determine whether that territory would be slave or free. The Reverend Henry Ward Beecher openly solicited from his pulpit funds to buy "freedom rifles," and many other clergymen followed his example. The entire nation became agitated over the case of Dred Scott, a Missouri slave who sued for freedom on the grounds that he had lived for years in a free state and consequently was a free man. The Supreme Court consented to hear his case.

It was in this atmosphere that Mrs. Stowe began work on her new novel, loosely based on the 1831 slave insurrection in Virginia, which had been led by Nat Turner, a slave and lay preacher. She paid scant attention to the facts of the Turner uprising, instead of this approach turning the story of the revolt to her own purposes and subsequently responding to critics by maintaining that "fiction creates its own truths."

The original title was *Dread: A Tale of the Great Dismal Swamp,* and in a letter to the publisher Professor Stowe remarked that this name was "startling, suggestive, perfectly appropriate, full of meaning, and in the present aspect of our country's affairs, has a fearfully symbolic, prophetic sound." The author added a postscript in which she declared, "As things now are, the very title will sell thousands of copies. Dread is in reality the hero of the book, the Dismal Swamp the theatre."

By the time the novel was nearing completion, late in 1855, the entire nation was anxiously awaiting the decision of

Chief Justice Roger B. Taney and his associate justices in the case of *Dred Scott* vs. *Sanford*. Mrs. Stowe, no longer able to resist temptation, removed a single letter from the title of her book and called it *Dred*.

The novel was published in January, 1856, and its initial success was as great as that of *Uncle Tom's Cabin*. By April more than two hundred fifty thousand copies had been sold in the United States; in Great Britain, one hundred thousand copies had been sold in the first month. In March the Supreme Court ruled against Dred Scott, infuriating the North, delighting the South, and, incidentally, guaranteeing the continuing success of the book.

Reviewers in the North hailed the work as a masterpiece. English critics were equally generous, and Queen Victoria let it be known that she preferred *Dred* to *Uncle Tom's Cabin*. Posterity has been less kind, calling *Dred* effective antislavery propaganda and one of the worst of Mrs. Stowe's novels.

Her problem, seen in the perspective of a century and a quarter, is that she had exhausted herself emotionally in writing *Uncle Tom's Cabin*, and its successor was curiously flat. Much of her factual material was drawn from the *Key*, and the new work lacked both vitality and depth of characterization. In addition, Mrs. Stowe cast aside much of her moderation, and although she tried hard to present a few Southerners in balance, many were so evil they became caricatures.

Perhaps her failure stemmed for the most part from her ignorance of plantation life in Virginia and the Carolinas. In *Dred* she wrote in detail about a section of the country she had never visited, relying on her own imagination instead of personal acquaintance, and as a consequence *Dred* is a fantasy that lacks both spontaneity and a sense of reality.

The South, instead of growing indignant, merely laughed at the author and dismissed her novel as inconsequential. The North, sharing her hostility to slavery, applauded her work and bought copies by the hundreds of thousands. Foreign publishers again flocked to her, and translations appeared in more than thirty countries.

Regardless of *Dred*'s value as propaganda or lack of it as literature, royalties from its sales, combined with the author's continuing income from *Uncle Tom's Cabin*, placed her in a professional class by herself. She had more readers than any other writer in the United States, and her income was several times greater than those of her nearest rivals. When it was suggested to Charles Dickens, in London, that her popularity approached his, the great novelist graciously insisted that her readership was much larger.

Mrs. Stowe kept financial records haphazardly, her husband jotted figures on scraps of paper and the backs of envelopes, and neither ever really knew how much money she was making. As nearly as can be estimated, her royalties in 1856-60 averaged about six thousand dollars per month, roughly the equivalent of seven hundred fifty thousand dollars per year in the final decades of the twentieth century. At that time, a roast of beef for eight cost fifty cents, bread sold for a penny a loaf, the material for a lady's silk dress could be purchased for a dollar or less, and servant girls, in addition to their room and board, received wages of two dollars per month. A student at Harvard College paid tuition of fifty dollars per year, and the heads of major corporations, including steel companies, shipping concerns, and fabric mills, received salaries of about ten thousand dollars per year. Harriet Beecher Stowe was wealthy beyond belief, well on her way toward becoming the first millionaire author in American history.

She remained unchanged in her way of life, however, refusing to buy a carriage and a team of horses, saying she could not afford the upkeep, and, when visiting New York, she preferred to stay with the Henry Ward Beechers in Brooklyn rather that pay an exorbitant $1.50 per day for a suite in a Manhattan hotel. Money, she was fond of saying, meant no more to her than it had when she was poor. To a large extent she was right, but she no longer had to worry about poverty and, when she wished, she could indulge herself in an occasional whim.

One whim particularly attracted her. She wanted to make another trip to Europe, especially to Great Britain, so that she could renew her friendships with the many ladies and gentlemen with whom she continued to correspond at great length. Her older children were now able to appreciate the benefits of foreign culture, and she decided she would take her twin daughters and Henry, who was then eighteen years old. Professor Stowe would accompany her, of course, but if she decided to linger for a time on the Continent after he found it necessary to return for the autumn term at the Andover Theological Seminary, she needed another companion. Her sister Mary Perkins was available and willing, her own children having reached adulthood.

The party of six sailed from New York on a steamer late in June, 1856, and reached Liverpool in mid-July. Mrs. Stowe carried a special case filled with seasickness remedies, but the weather was perfect and she had no need of them on the voyage. The family's first destination was Inverary Castle, where they would be the guests of the Duke and Duchess of Argyll. A special thrill awaited Mrs. Stowe on the journey there.

Queen Victoria, who had read both of her novels, had become her ardent admirer and wanted to meet her. Royal etiquette made it impossible for a public invitation to be extended to the Americans because they had not been formally presented at court, but there were more ways than one to set up a meeting, and an "accidental" encounter was arranged on the platform of a small railroad station where the two families "happened" to be changing trains.

The Stowe children remained in the background, as did four of the children of the Queen. How Mrs. Perkins occupied herself is not known. Professor Stowe bowed, Prince Albert bowed; Professor Stowe bowed, Prince Albert bowed. According to Stowe, each repeated the gesture four times, but his wife counted five each.

The two most influential ladies in the Anglo-Saxon world measured each other, and each liked what she saw. Mrs. Stowe curtsied rather clumsily, Victoria lifted her to her feet, and within moments they were whispering and giggling like a pair of schoolgirls. They stood apart from the others, so no one overheard their conversation, and Mrs. Stowe, mindful of the demands of royalty, subsequently revealed no details of their talk except that the Queen had promised they would meet again.

The Stowe party stayed at Inverary Castle for about a week and thoroughly enjoyed the visit. Every morning at nine o'clock, immediately before breakfast, the duke read selections from the Bible and offered prayers in the great dining hall. The duchess and her nine children sat in the center of the hall, with the guests seated in a row at one side. Facing them were the many uniformed servants, who stood. Mrs. Stowe was deeply impressed by the piety of her hosts.

Professor Stowe then hurried on to London, where he made arrangements for the British publication of *Dred* and obtained a copyright for the book. This formality had been neglected before the London publication of *Uncle Tom's Cabin*, causing a number of legal complications, and the Stowes had no intention of repeating the mistake. As soon as the professor's business was completed, he sailed back to the United States.

Mrs. Stowe, her sister, and the children went on to Dunrobin Castle, about sixty miles from Inverary, for a stay with the equally pious Duke and Duchess of Sutherland. There were daily prayers there, too, and long daily discussions of religion.

At Dunrobin a major cause of worry for Mrs. Stowe was relieved. Henry, beset by adolescent rebellion, had resisted the efforts of his parents to enroll him as a church member, and his mother was secretly afraid he had agnostic leanings. She was delighted, however, when she saw he filled his goblet with water every night for the long exchange of toasts in which gentlemen indulged. Any youth who shunned spirits and confined his drinking to water, she wrote to her husband, was certain to find God, and she felt infinitely better about Henry's approaching term at Dartmouth College.

An incident that took place during Mrs. Stowe's stay at

Dunrobin indicates her lack of understanding of the British aristocracy and the sources of its income. A number of anonymous letters awaited her, apparently written in concert, and these were soon followed by similar letters to the press. Mrs. Stowe, they declared, claimed she was the champion of the slave, but she was also the good friend of British slave owners and therefore mocked her own principles. It was beyond Mrs. Stowe's comprehension that Sutherland and others like him owned coal mines in the Midlands and paid the miners semistarvation wages, and that the rents they charged their tenants were so high the farmers found it difficult to make ends meet. Thoroughly bewildered, she said her hosts were good Christians, considerate of everyone, and she dismissed the letter-writers from her mind as mischief-makers, demented, or both.

Another, more welcome, letter, from Lady Byron, awaited Mrs. Stowe at Dunrobin, filled with praise for *Dred* and containing a sentence that Mrs. Stowe later quoted on occasions she deemed appropriate. "If there is truth in what I heard Lord Byron say, that works of fiction *lived* only by the amount of *truth* which they contained, your story is sure of long life." The two ladies promised to meet at the first opportunity, and both looked forward to the occasion.

Traveling by easy stages to London after leaving Dunrobin, and breaking the journey by staying for a day or two with various friends, Mrs. Stowe said good-bye to her son at York, as he had to be home in time for the beginning of his college career. Then, when she was only a day out of London, Mrs. Stowe received an invitation to dine with Queen Victoria at Windsor Castle that same evening. Only the Queen and Prince Albert were present, she later related, and they ate in a small dining room "off ordinary chinaware." The meal itself was far from sumptuous, consisting of a few dishes plainly cooked.

Prince Albert was pleasantly polite but took little part in the conversation and withdrew at the end of the meal. Victoria and her guest repaired to a small sitting room, and the Queen discussed *Dred* and *Uncle Tom's Cabin* in great detail, revealing the passages that had caused her to weep. Her knowledge of Americans in general and the Beechers in particular was astonishing to Mrs. Stowe. She knew many details of Lyman Beecher's career, inquiring closely after his health, and she was also familiar with Henry Ward Beecher's great success in Brooklyn. She was a gentle, quiet woman with "a strong sense of morality," and it was difficult for her guest to remember she was the ruler of the largest and most powerful empire on earth.

The tone of Mrs. Stowe's letters to her husband indicates that, no matter how great her belief in equality for all, she enjoyed her relations with Queen, dukes, and duchesses. She made no apology for her attitude; if she was a trifle snobbish in her friendships, she had earned that right.

Before reaching London, Mrs. Stowe received another letter from Lady Byron, which contained a check for fifty pounds, to be donated to "the sufferers in Kansas." Mrs. Stowe's reply reflects the progress of their friendship.

> How glad I was to see your handwriting once more! How more than glad I should be to see *you!* I do long to see you. I have so much to say,—so much to ask, and need to be refreshed with a sense of a congenial and sympathetic soul.
>
> Thank you, my dear friend, for your sympathy with our poor sufferers in Kansas. May God bless you for it! By doing this you will step to my side; perhaps you may share something of that abuse which they who "know not what they do" heap upon all who so feel for the right. I assure you, dear friend, I am *not* insensible to the fiery darts which thus fly around me....
>
> Direct as usual to my publishers, and believe me, as ever, with all my heart,
>
> Affectionately yours,
>
> H. B. S.

It is possible, although Mrs. Stowe probably failed to

realize it, that she was searching for a new confidante. A short time before her departure from Massachusetts, she had received a sad farewell letter from her lifelong friend Georgiana May Sykes, who had just been told by her physicians that she would not recover from a serious illness. Harriet Beecher Stowe, who had used her as an emotional sounding board for many years, grieved, and needed someone to replace her. She had not yet become intimate with Lady Byron, for whom she felt such affinity, but was moving in that direction.

After a visit of several days with Charles Kingsley, Mrs. Stowe and her party went on to London, spiritually refreshed after holding long theological discussions with the clergyman. Mrs. Perkins and the twins spent the better part of their time sightseeing, and Mrs. Stowe visited various friends. Accustomed now to her fame, she wanted no repetition of the social whirl that had kept her so busy on her first trip to England. At her request, no parties were given in her honor, and she enjoyed a number of quiet lunches, teas, and dinners with friends. If she saw Lady Byron during her sojourn—and no specific information is available on the subject—they may have met once or twice at tea.

The sedate pace suited her temperament, and she found it gratifying to be accepted for herself. Apparently she did not recognize that, although she was a member of a large family, she had been lonely most of her life. In England her friendships were civilized, even a trifle remote, in keeping with her own reserved nature.

Slavery, religion, and literature were the principal topics of conversation at most gatherings, Mrs. Stowe showing no discernible interest in either American or British politics. In none of her correspondence did she mention the presidential election of 1856 that sent former Secretary of State and senator James Buchanan of Pennsylvania to the White House. She seems to have had no idea how slavery might be abolished in practical terms. She saw it as an evil that required eradication, but detailed methods were beyond her grasp. It was not until the outbreak of Civil War hostilities, in

1861, that she began to take an active interest in day-to-day news.

She was pleased when her English friends displayed familiarity with the works of American authors, among them Longfellow, Hawthorne, and Poe. It disturbed her that James Russell Lowell, her friend, was less well known. She carried some of his poetry with her, and in a letter to her husband she asked that he be sure to tell Lowell that she had read some of his work aloud at a small social gathering.

During her stay in England, Mrs. Stowe had a meeting with John Ruskin, then thirty-seven years old and just beginning to acquire a reputation as an author and critic. She made no mention of the incident, so there is no way of knowing what she thought of him, but he wrote about the meeting in detail. His attitude was faintly patronizing, even though they shared enthusiasms for Gothic architecture and the works of Sir Walter Scott. Ruskin, responsible in larger measure than anyone else for the soaring reputation of Joseph Turner, the great romantic landscape artist who had died in 1851, proudly showed the visitor his gallery of Turner paintings. Mrs. Stowe indicated that she remained loyal to Rubens and Rembrandt. Ruskin escorted her to Durham for a stay of several hours and was amused because she elected to take a boat ride on the river rather than inspect some rare manuscripts in the cathedral library. He found it inexplicable that an author of stature could prefer the river view to an old manuscript.

On November 6, 1856, Mrs. Stowe, Mrs. Perkins, and the twins arrived in Paris, intending to stay for the winter so they could study French. They took up residence at the home of their teacher, a Mme. Borione, on the Rue de Clichy, and were comfortably ensconced in a parlor and two-bedroom suite. Twenty-one people in all were living in the place, all of them fellow students, and most of them Americans. Only French was spoken under Mme. Borione's roof, and formal lessons took up the better part of each morning.

Mrs. Stowe's love affair with Paris continued, and she confessed she would be content to spend the rest of her life there. She particularly enjoyed her aimless strolls through the city, when she often paused at a shop to buy an inexpensive gift for the children at home, or sat on a park bench to watch youngsters at play. She approved of the atmosphere in the home of Mme. Borione, a Protestant, because time was set aside each day for Bible readings and prayers.

Dred was also being published in Paris, and Mrs. Stowe's French publisher would not allow her to escape all of her obligations as an author. She was required to sit as a model for a bust in marble, and she paid a ceremonial visit to a school to accept a contribution to the antislavery cause from children who had read *Uncle Tom's Cabin.*

A number of ladies at whose homes discussion groups were regularly held opened their doors to Mrs. Stowe, and she accepted the invitations of three, a Mme. Mohl, a Mme. Lanziel, and again a Mme. Belloc. This meant, as she explained to her husband in a letter, that she could make visits and meet friends three evenings a week, if she chose to go out that much. "All these salôns are informal, social gatherings," she said, "with no fuss of refreshments, no nonsense of any kind. Just the cheeriest, heartiest, kindest little receptions you ever saw."

This mid-nineteenth century puritan approved of Paris in general, too, because she felt that externals did not indicate the true nature of the French people. "A kiss to dear little Charley," she told Professor Stowe. "If he could see all the things that I see every day in the Tuileries and Champs Elysées, he would go wild. All Paris is a general whirligig out of doors, but indoors people seem steady, quiet, and sober as anybody."

Some of the other observations on life in Paris she related to her husband are equally illuminating.

> This is Sunday evening, and a Sunday in Paris always puts me in mind of your story about somebody who said, "Bless you! They make such a noise that the Devil couldn't meditate!" All the extra work and odd jobs of life are put into Sunday. Your washerwoman comes Sunday, with her innocent, good-humored face, and would be infinitely at a loss to know why she shouldn't. Your

bonnet, cloak, shoes, and everything are sent home Sunday morning, and all the way to church there is such whirligiging and pirouetting along the boulevards as almost takes one's breath away....

I must say, life in Paris is arranged more sensibly than with us. Visiting involves no trouble in the feeding line. People don't go to eat. A cup of tea and plate of biscuit is all,—just enough to break up the stiffness.

It is wonderful that the people here do not seem to have got over "Uncle Tom" a bit. The impression seems as fresh as if just published. How often have they said, That book has revived the Gospel among the poor of France; it has done more than all the books we have published put together. It has gone among the *les ouvriers,* among the poor of Faubourg St. Antoine, and nobody knows how many have been led to Christ by it. Is this not blessed, my dear husband? Is it not worth all the suffering of writing it?

Mrs. Stowe found the response of Paris literary critics to *Dred* encouraging. *La Presse,* the largest and most influential newspaper in the city, gave it an exceptionally favorable review, as did *Revue des Deux Mondes,* which also printed several long excerpts from the book. In spite of the enormous sale in Great Britain, the *London Times,* the *Athenaeum,* and the imposing *Edinburgh Review* had treated *Dred* with harsh disrespect, and the contrasting kindness of the Parisian critics impelled Mrs. Stowe to remark, "Generally speaking, French critics seem to have a finer appreciation of my subtle shades of meaning than English."

Her command of French improving steadily, Mrs. Stowe soon found it possible to converse with ease. Foreign languages did not come readily to her, but she achieved her goal and was satisfied. The time had come to resume her travels.

She placed her twin daughters in a Protestant boarding school in Paris, intending to leave them there until she returned, on her way home. They did so well at the school, however, acquiring a patina of culture, and becoming "as French as the French themselves," that they were allowed to remain for two years.

On February 1, 1857, Mrs. Stowe and her sister departed for Rome, traveling through France at a leisurely pace, making stops in Amiens, Lyons, and Marseilles. There they took a steamer, which made stops at Genoa and Leghorn, but they were delayed by a collision with another vessel before debarking at Civitavecchia. Their run of bad luck continued, for after a two-hour delay over passports the sisters hired a carriage to take them to Rome, and it lost a wheel on a lonely stretch of road. The repairs took another hour, and then the horses went out of control. At each stop the driver demanded more money than the agreed upon price, and the carriage was surrounded by a mob that "raved and ranted at us till finally we paid much more than we ought, to get rid of them." The passport officer at the gates of Rome had to be bribed, too, and at two in the morning the weary sisters drove into Rome, only to find that no accommodations were available at any of the five hotels they tried.

Then the wheel fell off the carriage again, and another crowed gathered, several urchins trying to run off with the luggage. The visitors were afraid they would be forced to spend the entire night in the streets, but another carriage appeared and, with the crowd following, took the two Americans to a boardinghouse owned by a woman who spoke French. Mrs. Stowe and her sister were somewhat reassured but searched their room for "treacherous testers or trapdoors." Finding none, they went off to sleep in a "very clean, white bed." The following day they moved to the comfortable apartment that had been prepared for them.

This thoroughly unpleasant experience, combined with the sisters' suspicions, ingrained since earliest childhood, of the capital of Catholicism, convinced them they would hate Rome. Instead, like so many visitors over the centuries, they fell in love with the place. In a letter written to her husband on March 1, Mrs. Stowe expressed her enthusiasm in no uncertain terms.

> Every day is opening to me a new world of wonders here in
> Italy. I have been to the Catacombs, where I was shown

many memorials of the primitive Christians, and today we are going to the Vatican. The weather is sunny and beautiful beyond measure, and flowers are springing in the fields on every side. Oh, my dear, how I do long to have you here to enjoy what you are so much better fitted to appreciate than I,—this wonderful combination of the past and present, of what has been and what is!

Think of strolling leisurely through the Forum, of seeing the very stones that were laid in the time of the Republic, of rambling over the ruined palace of the Caesars, of walking under the Arch of Titus, of seeing the Dying Gladiator, and whole ranges of rooms filled with wonders of art, all in one morning! All this I did on Saturday, and only wanted you. You know so much more and could appreciate so much better. At the Palace of the Caesars, where the very dust is a *mélange* of exquisite marbles, I saw for the first time an acanthus growing, and picked my first leaf....

Rome is a world! Rome is an astonishment! Papal Rome is an enchantress! Old as she is, she is like Ninon d'Enclos,—the young fall in love with her.

After tearing themselves away from Rome, Mrs. Stowe and Mrs. Perkins went to Naples, where they engaged in the usual obligatory sightseeing, visiting Pompeii and Herculaneum, and climbing Vesuvius. Mrs. Stowe described the volcano in great detail in a letter she wrote to her daughters in Paris, and said it reminded her of "Milton's description of the infernal places."

Retracing their steps, the sisters traveled by a small ship from Naples to Leghorn, then went on to Florence for a stay of two weeks. There, Mrs. Stowe sent a note to Robert and Elizabeth Barrett Browning, asking to see them. Browning's work was as yet not widely read, and he was little understood, but his wife was at the height of her popularity, regarded by many, especially romantic ladies, as the greatest of living poets writing in English.

The Brownings were not overjoyed at the prospect of entertaining the author of *Uncle Tom's Cabin,* although Mrs. Browning admitted the novel had accomplished much good.

Mrs. Stowe was a puritan, and they were certain they would be bored by her religious disputations. Bad enough that she was an American; worse, she was a provincial American. She was also a reformer, which meant she would be aggressive and assertive. The couple steeled themselves for her visit, telling each other they could endure anything for an hour.

To their astonishment, the Brownings were captivated by Harriet Beecher Stowe, and at their insistence she stayed for dinner and sat with them until late in the evening. They found her far more "refined" and sensitive, much less "American" than they had anticipated. She was also much more attractive than her portraits had led them to believe, and, in her manner, so simple and earnest that she seemed completely unaware of her fame.

That visit was the beginning of a long friendship. Mrs. Stowe returned to the Browning home repeatedly during her stay in Florence, and the couple became her ardent admirers, finding literary qualities in her work that her more severe English critics failed to see. Later, letters were exchanged, and Robert Browning kept up the correspondence for many years after his wife's death. "I am proud to call Mrs. Stowe my good friend," he wrote, and she reciprocated the feeling.

The travelers next went on to Venice, which Mrs. Stowe regarded as the most romantic place she had ever seen. They stopped in Milan to see the cathedral and Leonardo da Vinci's *Last Supper,* resting at Lake Como before hurrying back to Rome. No longer afraid she would be "contaminated" by Catholicism, Mrs. Stowe wrote her impressions of Holy Week in Rome to her husband.

> Certainly no thoughtful or sensitive person, no person impressible either through the senses or the religious feelings, can fail to feel it deeply.
>
> In the first place, the mere fact of the different nations of the earth moving, so many of them, with one accord, to so old and venerable a city, to celebrate the death and resurrection of Jesus, is something in itself affecting. Whatever disputes there may be about the other commemorative feasts of Christendom, the time

of this epoch is fixed unerringly by the Jews' Passover. That great and solemn feast, therefore, stands as an historical monument to mark the date of the most important thrilling events which this world ever witnessed.

When one sees the city filling with strangers, pilgrims arriving on foot, the very shops decorating themselves in expectancy, every church arranging its services, the prices even of temporal matters raised by the crowd and its demands, he naturally thinks, Wherefore, why is all this? and he must be very careless indeed if it do not bring to mind, in a more real way than before, that at this very time, so many years ago, Christ and his apostles were living actors in the scenes thus celebrated today.

Leaving Rome the day after Easter, Mrs. Stowe and Mrs. Perkins went without delay to Paris, where they found the husband of their sister Isabella awaiting them. They enjoyed a family reunion for a few days, and Hooker, his business completed, proposed a holiday in Switzerland. But Mrs. Stowe had business of her own to attend to with her publishers in London, so she parted company with her sister and brother-in-law. After making arrangements to keep her daughters at school in Paris because "a few months more of study here will do them a world of good," she made plans to sail for home from Liverpool on the steamer *Europa,* which was scheduled to leave on June 6.

She was homesick for her husband and younger children after her long holiday, but she was eager to see Lady Byron in London before rejoining them.

11

Lady Byron was a woman with an unhappy past, as anyone acquainted with the story of her stormy marriage well knew. Annabella Milbanke, only daughter of Sir Ralph and Lady Judith Milbanke, had the misfortune to be the niece of Lady Melbourne, who was confidante of the mercurial poet, freedom fighter, champion of liberal causes, and libertine. After youthful affairs with Lady Melbourne's daughter-in-law, Lady Caroline Lamb, Lady Frances Webster, and his own half-sister, Augusta Leigh, among others, Byron met the innocent, serious-minded Annabella, and the novelty of her personality intrigued him.

She was persuaded by Lady Melbourne to marry him, and did, in January, 1815. In December of that year, she gave birth to his daughter, and the following month she returned to the home of her parents, ostensibly for a visit, after one year and three days of marriage. A few days later, Sir Ralph informed an astonished Byron that his wife had left him and had no intention of seeing him again, much less of returning to him. No reason, public or private, was given for the break, but presumably Byron understood.

Lady Byron remained steadfast in her determination to have nothing more to do with her husband, in spite of the efforts of various friends to arrange a reconciliation. Her mourning was perfunctory after Byron's hero's death in 1824, in Greece, where he had gone to aid the cause of that country's independence.

Wealthy in her own right as well as through an inheritance from her husband, Lady Byron lived quietly in London and her country home, turning increasingly to religion, giving generously to various charities, and avoiding the limelight. She remained a living symbol for those who worshiped her husband, whose reputation as a poet continued to grow after his death; to save herself from embarrassment she retired more and more into illnesses, both real and imagined. Many people regarded her as eccentric, and there were some who said she suffered from occasional periods of madness.

By the time Harriet Beecher Stowe returned to England in the spring of 1857, Lady Byron had been a widow for thirty-three years and was still forced to endure the light of her husband's reflected glory. Certainly Mrs. Stowe was one of his warm, lifelong admirers and made no secret of her feelings.

"I look upon creeds of all kinds as chains," Lady Byron wrote to her American friend, "far worse chains than those you would break, as the cause of much hypocrisy and infidelity. I may not have time to grow wiser; and I must therefore leave it to others to correct the conclusions I have now formed from my life's experience. I should be happy to discuss them personally with you; for it would be *soul to soul*."

Mrs. Stowe was overwhelmed, excited beyond measure by the prospect of forming a deep friendship with the widow of the man who had written *Childe Harold*. Lady Byron was confined to her bed but graciously consented to see her whenever it was convenient to call, and Mrs. Stowe hastily took care of her business with her publishers before presenting herself at her hostess's town house.

Describing the sickroom, Mrs. Stowe later wrote that beside the invalid's bed "stood a table covered with books, pamphlets, and files of letters, all arranged with exquisite order...Lady Byron still directed with systematic care, her various works of benevolence, and watched with intelligent attention the course of science, literature, and religion; and the versatility and activity of her mind, the flow of brilliant and penetrating thought on all the topics of the day, gave to the conversations of her retired room a peculiar charm."

The two ladies discussed *Dred*, the bloodshed in Kansas, and related topics, and inevitably began to talk about Lord Byron. Mrs. Stowe was eager to hear more about him. At their next meeting, a few days later, Lady Byron "seemed pleased to continue the subject and went on to say many things of his singular character and genius, more penetrating and more appreciative than is often met with among critics."

In reply, Mrs. Stowe said that she "had been from childhood powerfully influenced by him," and began to relate how she had prayed for his soul as a child of thirteen. Lady Byron interrupted to say she had already heard the story and that "it was one of the things that made me wish to *know* you. I think *you* could understand him." Harriet Beecher Stowe felt that no more flattering remark could have been made to her.

She was invited to the house yet again, this time for a luncheon, the invalid managing to haul herself down the stairs. Also present was her grandson, Lord Ockham, and Lady Byron analyzed his eccentricities with "benevolence and tolerance."

Before Mrs. Stowe departed for home, Lady Byron invited her once more to call, saying that she wished to speak alone with her friend on a subject of importance. When the guest arrived, she found that this was one of her hostess's "well days"; she moved "with her usual air of quiet simplicity...full of little acts of consideration for all about her." Two other ladies, apparently good friends, were also present, but Lady Byron excused herself and took her American friend to a small sitting room.

There they remained closeted for an entire afternoon, and Lady Byron at last revealed her true opinion of her late husband, a man who had been taught to revere the Bible but who had written the scurrilous *Don Juan*. Society, to be sure, was to blame for much that had happened to him. He had sinned, like so many people, and had admitted his sins, but society had cast him out. Lady Byron declared that she had been willing to forget his many affairs, some of which he had flaunted in public. After all, he was behaving no differently than other young English aristocrats. But there was one sin Lady Byron could not forgive. "Mrs. Stowe, he was guilty of incest with his sister!" The New England lady was so shocked she could not speak.

Lady Byron was not yet finished. A new, inexpensive edition of her late husband's works was about to be published and would be bought in quantity by ordinary people. England had already been demoralized by his glamorous lies, and now it would become even more corrupt. Lady Byron wondered whether it was her duty to reveal her dreadful secret to the world and thus prevent Byron from perpetrating still more evil from his grave.

When asked her opinion, Mrs. Stowe did not know what to say; they discussed the problem at length but came to no conclusion.

When Mrs. Stowe departed she carried with her the firm conviction that Lady Byron was the most noble-hearted woman who had ever lived. It was a view she never changed. For years Harriet Beecher Stowe wondered whether she should be the one to reveal Lady Byron's horrible secret to the world. On many occasions, she talked about the matter with her husband, who urged caution, a response she did not want to hear. She also discussed it with Mary Perkins, the most sophisticated of her immediate realtives, and Mrs. Perkins's advice was as sound as it was blunt: Let Lady Byron tell her own story. Anyone else who told it would bring castastrophe and shame on her own head. The world simply was not prepared to hear such a tale.

It is difficult to believe that Mrs. Stowe could have been so naive, but nothing in her experience had prepared her for Lady Byron's revelation about a man Harriet Beecher had idolized.

She was particularly ingenuous in accepting her friend's statement that she alone had been told the secret. Certainly she should have realized that Lady Byron was eccentric and that a story told to a semistranger also had been revealed to others. Apparently it did not occur to her that the neurotic Lady Byron was trying to win her undeviating sympathy. As a matter of fact, the story of Byron's affair with Augusta Leigh had been known to a number of people, not the least of them Lady Byron's aunt, Lady Melbourne, who had encouraged him to initiate other affairs in order to bring his dangerous liaison to an end.

On an earlier occasion, Mrs. Stowe had seen her friend in what others called one of her "frozen fits," but the American interpreted the condition as a variation of her own fatigue.

> She could not see me at first; and when, at last she came, it was evident that she was in a state of utter prostration. Her hands were like ice; her face was deadly pale; and she conversed with a constraint and difficulty which showed what exertion it was for her to keep up at all....
> In a state of health which would lead most persons to become helpless absorbents of services from others, she was assuming burdens, and making outlays of her vital powers in acts of love and service, with a generosity that often reduced her to utter exhaustion. But none who knew or loved her ever misinterpreted the coldness of those seasons of exhaustion. We knew that it was *not* the spirit that was chilled, but only the frail mortal tabernacle.

Having convinced herself that her friend's condition was exclusively physical, Mrs. Stowe saw no reason to be on her guard, and acted accordingly. She spent her last day in London with Lady Byron, who rallied sufficiently for the occasion to take a long carriage ride, to stroll through a park, and to drink tea in a hotel. Writing from Liverpool immediately before sailing for home, Mrs. Stowe reveals the depth of her attachment to Lady Byron in a letter that has a breathless, schoolgirl flavor, a quality she was herself quick to recognize:

Dear Friend,—I left you with a strange sort of yearning, throbbing feeling—you make me feel quite as I did
years ago, a sort of girlishness quite odd for me. I have
felt a strange longing to send you something. Don't smile
when you see what it turns out to be. I have a weakness
for your pretty Parian things; it is one of my own home
peculiarities to have strong passions for pretty tea-cups
and other little matters for my own quiet meals, when,
as often happens, I am too unwell to join the family. So
I send you a cup made of primroses, a funny little pit-
cher, quite large enough for cream, and a little vase for
violets and primroses—which will be lovely together—and
when you use it think of me and that I love you more
than I can say.

I often think how strange it is that I should *know*
you—you who were a sort of legend of my early days—
that I should love you is only a natural result. You seem
to me to stand on the confines of that land where the
poor formalities which separate hearts here pass like
mist before the sun, and therefore it is that I feel the
language of love must not startle you as strange or
unfamiliar. You are so nearly there in spirit that I fear
with every adieu that it may be the last; yet did you pass
within the veil I should not feel you lost.

I have got past the time when I feel that my heavenly
friends are *lost* by going there. I feel them *nearer*, rather
than farther off.

So good-by, dear, dear friend, and if you see morning
in our Father's house before I do, carry my love to those
that wait for me, and if I pass first, you will find me there,
and we shall love each other *forever*.

Mrs. Stowe remained true to her trust, as she saw it, and
when Lady Byron did not reveal her secret herself, she became
increasingly convinced that it was her Christian duty to make
the sensational story public. It was the least she could do in
"the sacred name of friendship," and her conviction firmed
over the years until it became an irresistible compulsion. In the
meanwhile, there were other battles to be fought, other
triumphs to win, other losses to suffer.

The preoccupation with death that Mrs. Stowe displayed in her letter to Lady Byron was not typical of her. Always concerned with God's love for man and man's need to live accordingly, she was rarely morbid. Although Professor Stowe was psychic, or claimed to be, and the whole family believed he frequently sensed or knew about events before they happened, his wife had never shown any such tendencies; yet death was very much on her mind during her Atlantic crossing, and although the weather was fair and the sea calm she spent much of her time alone in her cabin.

Her forebodings were forgotten when she reached home at the end of June after an absence of almost a year and was reunited with her husband and children. Only the twins and Henry were absent, the former still attending school in Paris, the latter completing his freshman year at Dartmouth. He wrote that he would come home about the middle of the month, after taking his final examinations. Until then, in spite of his heavy academic schedule, he was keeping in shape by hiking in the woods beyond the Hanover, New Hampshire, campus of Dartmouth College and swimming in the Connecticut River.

On July 10 Professor and Mrs. Stowe received word that Henry had drowned in the river the previous day. Both were crushed, and some members of the family believed that the professor never completely recovered from the shock. His wife proved her mettle by forcing herself to accept the inevitable and within two weeks was able to answer letters of condolence and to write freely to friends in England and elsewhere about the tragedy. There was no self-pity, no hint of the morbid in her attitude. Henry Ward Beecher hurried to Andover from Brooklyn when he heard the news, but his sister was beyond the reach of his comfort. Only time would heal her grief; meanwhile, her faith in the Almighty remained strong, and sustained her. And she was the rock on whom her other children and her husband leaned.

"I am submissive, but not reconciled," Professor Stowe said, and three or four times each day visited his son's grave, walking around it until weariness forced him to return to the house to rest. For his sake, Mrs. Stowe pretended she needed a change, and in September they went up to Brunswick, Maine, taking the younger children with them. There they swam, went on picnics, visited old friends, and took long walks on the beach. By the time they returned to Andover at the end of September the professor's balance was at least partly restored and he was ready to resume his duties at the seminary. His wife took refuge in work.

In November, 1857, Harriet Beecher Stowe contributed an allegorical story, "The Mourning Veil," to a new magazine published in Boston, the *Atlantic Monthly*. This was the beginning of an association that lasted for the rest of her active career, and the *Atlantic* became the principal outlet for her shorter fiction as well as her articles. Indeed, the luster of her name, the virtual guarantee that an issue containing a piece by her would sell out, was a major factor in the magazine's initial success.

James Russell Lowell, the *Atlantic*'s first editor, had great admiration for his friend's talents, and gave her carte blanche granted no one else, although most of the prominent authors of the day became contributors. Mrs. Stowe had the privilege of writing on any subject she wished, and her words were printed without change. From the outset, Lowell deliberately challenged the supremacy of a magazine founded seven years earlier in New York, *Harper's New Monthly*, which featured serializations of new English novels illustrated with woodcuts. Lowell's aim was to establish the periodical's greater literary stature, and many believed he achieved his goal because Mrs.

Stowe remained faithful to him. Henry Ward Beecher also became a contributor to the *Atlantic*, thanks to his sister's influence with Lowell, and in the process increased his own renown.

In the late autumn of 1857 and the early months of the following year, Mrs. Stowe settled down in earnest to write two novels more or less simultaneously, occasionally turning aside from both of them to produce a short story or an article. In her unhappiness, work was her only salvation; she was afraid she would brood about Henry's death, revealing her "weakness" to the world, if she wrote at a more sedate pace.

For the first time, she chose subjects other than the slavery issue for major pieces of fiction, and she was completely at home with both themes. *The Minister's Wooing*, first published in serialized form in the *Atlantic*, beginning with the December, 1858, issue and continuing for a year, dealt with the Protestant clergy of New England, a subject on which she was an undisputed expert. A romance, as the title indicates, the tale was also an examination of the struggles of ministers to save their own souls as well as those of their parishioners. It was filled, too, with the pros and cons of theological disputes that had echoed in her ears throughout her life. Despite its complexities, *The Minister's Wooing* was dictated to a secretary, the first book Mrs. Stowe had not written in her own hand. Her son, Charles, said in his mother's biography that the greater part of the book was prepared "under a great pressure of mental excitement."

The second work of this period, *The Pearl of Orr's Island*, was pastoral, something of a return to her early New England character studies, and dealt with the quiet natives of Maine she had come to know during her sojourn in Brunswick. Mrs. Stowe had been planning it for years and was aided by her notes, "more than enough in themselves to fill a book." She did the actual writing herself, and not only enjoyed the experience but, according to her son, found it relaxing. *The Pearl* first appeared in serial form in the *New York Independent*, also running in 1858, but Mrs. Stowe discovered she had too little time and was spreading herself too thin. She resolved her dilemma by calling her initial efforts "Part I," and promised that the second portion would be finished in the near future. Other matters intervened, however, and the completed novel was not published until 1862.

In a letter to Mrs. Stowe written many years later, in 1874, John Greenleaf Whittier, may have best expressed the public's reaction to the two novels. "When I am in the mood for thinking deeply I read 'The Minister's Wooing,'" he said. "But 'The Pearl of Orr's Island' is my favorite. It is the most charming New England idyl ever written."

The setting of *The Minister's Wooing* was Newport, Rhode Island, in the eighteenth century. The minister of the title, Samuel Hopkins, obviously based on Lyman Beecher, was a believer in the American theologian Jonathan Edwards's New Divinity. Leading a pure, blameless life, he struggled to achieve spiritual independence, at the same time attempting to assert his authority over a congregation that paid lip service to religion, merely observing church rules. He was endowed with a "grand humanity" that caused him, far ahead of his time, to oppose slavery and the slave trade. His greatest miscalculation was that of believing he could accomplish his ends by means of a more fervent preaching of the Gospel.

The lady he wooed was Mary Scudder, a typically Harriet Beecher Stowe heroine, almost too good to be true. Long-suffering and a model of resignation, she was, like the author, dedicated to the belief that God is love. Hopkins wooed her in vain because she had had only one love in her life, James Marvyn, a sailor who had been lost at sea. Mrs. Stowe's obvious inspiration for this part of her plot was the life of her sister Catherine, although it has been suggested that Catherine Beecher may not have been her only model. She may have seen herself in the role, grieving for her lost son Henry; she may also have had in mind Lady Byron, a lifelong sorrow locked within her heart.

Hopkins was convinced that James was condemned to eternal damnation unless he had been saved, just prior to his death, by a "miracle of regeneration." Mrs. Marvyn, his mother, suffered dreadfully, in rebellion against a cruel God who would ordain such a fate but was saved by Mary and her black servant, Candace, who was, of course, a free woman. They were able to convince her that God is love, thus enabling her to rise above her sorrow. As a final touch, the worldly and sophisticated James came home a convert to Christianity, and the mansion overlooking the Newport waterfront in which he and Mary settled for the rest of their lives was "more holy than cloister, more saintly and pure than church or altar—*a Christian home.*"

A relatively minor character in the book reflects Mrs. Stowe's new tolerance for Catholicism, which grew out of her long sojourns in Paris and Italy: the beautiful and vivacious Virginie de Frontignac, a romantic dreamer, wife of a French diplomat, who fell in love with one Aaron Burr. Mary not only helped Virginie to save her marriage but recalled Burr to his duty, and Virginie reciprocated by helping to bring Mary and James together.

Virginie's real function in the story was to demonstrate the good to be found in Roman Catholicism. In passage after long passage, interminable to the twentieth-century reader, Mary and Virginie engage in discussions that are, in effect, a comparative study of religions. The hells of Presbyterian and Catholic were found to be remarkably similar, both faiths stressed the need for atonement, and, in both, man found God through Christ. Mrs. Stowe even took a giant, daring stride toward modern liberalism, almost unthinkable in a daughter of Lyman Beecher, by showing that Protestant and Catholic each believed her friend could not find salvation except in the "One True Church," but that both in reality saved their souls because of their conviction that God is love.

Though Mary Scudder cannot be accepted as a three-dimensional character, she represents all that Mrs. Stowe regarded as pure, noble, and beyond reproach in puritanism. Little of the author's own nature is seen in Mary, who did not resemble the acerbic, self-disciplined Catherine Beecher either. Mary's firm sweetness well may have been a quality the author attributed to her own mother; at any rate, Mrs. Stowe put entire passages of letters written by Roxanna Foote to Dr. Beecher into Mary's mouth.

Aaron Burr, of course, was based on the real-life Vice-President of the United States, whose fortunes went into rapid decline after he killed Alexander Hamilton in a duel. Despised by many of his contemporaries, he was regarded, on the eve of the Civil War, as something of a romantic, swashbuckling adventurer. Mrs. Stowe portrayed him in that light and delighted in the regeneration her character underwent through the intervention of Mary Scudder. The real Aaron Burr, like her character, had been the grandson of Jonathan Edwards, and in her novel Mrs. Stowe strongly suggests that rigid theology, devoid of humanity, ultimately produces unscrupulous men because they have no conscience.

The Minister's Wooing, like all of Mrs. Stowe's books, was an overnight success. Published early in 1859, shortly after its serialization in the *Atlantic Monthly*, the book went through the pleasant, familiar process of being printed in edition after edition. It was equally successful in Great Britain, and within the next year translations appeared in twenty-three countries. Reviewers in the United States and critics abroad were in agreement that Mrs. Stowe had written her best, most profound work, James Russell Lowell discussed *The Minister's Wooing* at length in the *Atlantic*.

> It has always seemed to us that the anti-slavery element in the two former novels by Mrs. Stowe stood in the way of a full appreciation of her remarkable genius, at least in her own country. It was so easy to account for the unexampled popularity of "Uncle Tom" by attributing it to a cheap sympathy with sentimental philanthropy! As people began to recover from the first enchantment, they began to resent it and to complain that a dose of that insane Garrison-root which takes the reason prisoner had been palmed upon them without their knowing it, and that their ordinary water-gruel of fiction, thinned with sentiment and thickened with moral, had been hocussed with the bewildering hasheesh of Abolition. We had the advantage of reading that truly extraordinary book for the first time in Paris, long after the whirl of excitement produced by its publication had subsided, in the seclusion of distance, and

with a judgment unbiased by those political sympathies which it is impossible, perhaps unwise, to avoid at home. We felt then, and we believe now, that the secret of Mrs. Stowe's power lay in that same genius by which the great successes in creative literature have always been achieved,—the genius that instinctively goes right to the organic elements of human nature, whether under a white skin or a black, and which disregards as trivial the conventional and facetious notions which make so large a part both of our thinking and feeling. Works of imagination written with an aim to immediate impression are commonly ephemeral...but the creative faculty of Mrs. Stowe, like that of Cervantes in "Don Quixote" and of Fielding in "Joseph Andrews," overpowered the narrow specialty of her design, and expanded a local and temporary theme with the cosmopolitanism of genius.

It is a proverb that there is "a great deal of human nature in men," but it is equally and sadly true that there is amazingly little of it in books. Fielding is the only English novelist who deals with life in its broadest sense. Thackeray, his disciple and congener, and Dickens, the congener of Smollett, do not so much treat of life as the strata of society; the one studying nature from the club-room window, the other from the reporters' box in the police court. It may be that the general obliteration of distinctions of rank in this country, which is generally considered a detriment to the novelist, will in the end turn to his advantage by compelling him to depend for his effects on the contrasts and collisions in innate character, rather than on those shallow traits or super-induced by particular social arrangements, or by hereditary associations. Shakespeare drew ideal, and Fielding natural, men and women; Thackeray draws either gentlemen or snobs, and Dickens either unnatural men or the oddities natural only in the lowest grades of a highly artificial system of society. The first two knew human nature; of the two latter, one knows what is called the world, and the other the streets of London. Is it possible that the very social democracy which here robs the novelist of so much romance, so much costume, so much antithesis of caste, so much in short that is purely external, will give him a set-off in making it easier for him to get at that element of universal humanity which neither of the two extremes of an aristocratic system, nor the salient and picturesque points of contrast between the two, can alone lay open to him?

We hope to see this problem solved by Mrs. Stowe. That kind of romantic interest which Scott evolved from the relations of lord and vassal, of thief and clansman, from the social more than the moral contrast of Roundhead and Cavalier, of far-descended pauper and *nouveau riche* which Cooper found in the clash of savagery with civilization, and the shaggy virtue bred on the border-land between the two, Indian by habit, white by tradition, Mrs. Stowe seems in her former novels to have sought in a form of society alien to her sympathies, and too remote for exact study, or for the acquirement of that local truth which is the slow result of unconscious observation. There can be no stronger proof of the greatness of her genius, of her possessing that conceptive faculty which belongs to the higher order of imagination, than the avidity with which "Uncle Tom" was read at the South. It settled the point that this book was true to human nature, even if not minutely so to plantation life.

If capable of so great a triumph where success must so largely depend on the sympathetic insight of her mere creative power, have we not a right to expect something far more in keeping with the requirements of art, now that her wonderful eye is to be the mirror of familiar scenes, and if a society in which she was bred, of which she has seen so many varieties, and that, too, in the country, where it is most *naive* and original? It is a great satisfaction to us that in "The Minister's Wooing" she has chosen her time and laid her scene amid New England habits and traditions. There is no other writer who is capable of perpetuating for us, in a work of art, a style of thought and manners which railways and newspapers will soon render as plaeozoic as the mastodon or the megalosaurians. Thus far the story has fully justified our hopes. The leading characters are all fresh and individual creations. Mrs. Kate Scudder, the notable Yankee housewife; Mary, in whom Cupid is to try con-

clusions with Calvin; James Marvyn, the adventurous
boy of the coast, in whose heart the wild religion of
nature swells till the strait swathings of Puritanism are
burst; Dr. Hopkins, the conscientious minister come
upon a time when the social *prestige* of the clergy is
waning, and whose independence will test the voluntary
system of ministerial support; Simeon Brown, the man
of theological dialectics, in whom the utmost perfection
of creed is shown to be not inconsistent with the most
contradictory imperfection of life,—all these are characters new to fiction. And the scene is laid just far
enough away in point of time to give proper tone and
perspective.

We think we find in the story, so far as it has proceeded, the promise of an interest as unhackneyed as it
will be intense. There is room for the play of all the
passions and interests that make up the great tragi-
comedy of life, while all the scenery and accessories will
be those which familiarity has made dear to us. We are
a little afraid of Colonel Burr, to be sure, it is so hard to
make a historical personage fulfill the conditions demanded by the novel of every-day life. He is almost sure
either to fall below our traditional conception of him, or
to rise above the natural and easy level of character, into
the vague or melodramatic. Moreover, we do not want
a novel of society from Mrs. Stowe; she is quite too
good to be wasted in that way, and her tread is much
more firm on the turf of the "door-yard" or the pasture,
and the sanded floor of the farmhouse, than on the
velvet of the *salon*. We have no notion how she is to
develop her plot, but we think we foresee chances for her
best power in the struggle which seems foreshadowed
between Mary's conscientious admiration of the doctor
and her half-conscious passion for James, before she
discovers that one of these conflicting feelings means
simply moral liking and approval, and the other that she
is a woman and that she loves. And is not the value of
dogmatic theology as a rule of life to be thoroughly test-
ed for the doctor by his slave-trading parishioners? Is he
not to learn the bitter difference between intellectual
acceptance of a creed and that true partaking of the
sacrament of love and faith and sorrow that makes Christ

the very life-blood of our being and doing? And has not
James Marvyn also his lesson to be taught? We foresee
him gradually drawn back by Mary from his recoil
against Puritan formalism to a perception of how every
creed is pliant and plastic to a beautiful nature, of how
much charm there may be in an hereditary faith, even if it
have become almost conventional.

In the materials of character already present in the
story, there is scope for Mrs. Stowe's humor, pathos,
clear moral sense, and quick eye for the scenery of life.
We do not believe that there is any one who, by birth,
breeding and natural capacity, has had the opportunity
to know New England so well as she, or who has the
peculiar genius so to profit by the knowledge. Already
there have been scenes in "The Minister's Wooing"
that, in their lowness of tone and quiet truth, contrast as
charmingly with the humid vagueness of the modern
school of novel-writers as the "Vicar of Wakefield" itself, and we are greatly mistaken if it do not prove to be
the most characteristic of Mrs. Stowe's works, and
therefore that on which her fame will chiefly rest with
posterity.

Only in his belief that Mrs. Stowe would be remembered
more for her new work than for *Uncle Tom's Cabin* was
Lowell mistaken. The rest of his analysis is as valid over a century later as it was when he wrote it. Mrs. Stowe corresponded
with him about the book and treasured a letter he wrote to
her from his home in Cambridge, Massachusetts, on February
4, 1859, while the *Atlantic* was publishing the final portions.
He was simultaneously playful and serious, and she could not
doubt the sincerity of the poet for whom she had a greater
respect than for Longfellow, then regarded as America's first
writer. Lowell wrote:

> I certainly did mean to write you about your story, but only
> to cry *bravissima!* with the rest of the world. I intended
> no kind of criticism; deeming it wholly out of place, and
> in the nature of a wet-blanket, so long as a story is un-
> finished. When I got the first number in MS., I said to

Harriet Beecher Stowe

Mr. Phillips that I thought it would be the best thing you
had done, and what has followed has only confirmed
my first judgment. From long habit, and from the
tendency of my studies, I can not help looking at things
purely from an aesthetic point of view, and what *I* val-
ued in"Uncle Tom" was the genius, and not the moral.
That is saying a good deal, for I never use the word
genius at haphazard, and always (perhaps, too) spar-
ingly. I am going to be as frank as I ought to be with one
whom I value so highly. What especially charmed me
in the new story was, that you had taken your stand on
New England ground. You are one of the few persons
lucky enough to be born with eyes in your head,—that is,
with something behind the eyes which makes them of
value. To most people the seeing apparatus is as useless
as the great telescope at the observatory is to me,—something to stare through with no intelligent result. Nothing
could be better than the conception of your plot (so far
as I divine it), and the painting-in of your figures. As for
"theology," it is as much a part of daily life in New
England as in Scotland, and all I should have to say
about it is this: let it crop out when it naturally comes to
the surface, only don't dig down to it. A moral aim is a
fine thing, but in making a story an artist is a traitor who
does not sacrifice everything to art. Remember the
lesson that Christ gave us twice over. First, he preferred
the useless Mary to the dish-washing Martha, and next,
when that exemplary moralist and friend of humanity,
Judas, objected to the sinful waste of the Magdalen's
ointment, the great Teacher would rather it should be
wasted in an act of simple beauty than utilized for the
benefit of the poor. Cleopatra was an artist when she
dissolved her biggest pearl to captivate her Antony-
public. May I, a critic by profession, say the whole truth
to a woman of genius? Yes? And never be forgiven? I
shall try, and try to be forgiven, too. In the first place,
pay no regard to the advice of anybody, in the second
place, pay a great deal to mine! A Kilkenny-cattish style
of advice? Not at all. My advice is to follow your own
instincts,—to stick to nature, and to avoid what people
commonly call the "Ideal;" for that, and beauty, and

pathos, and success, all lie in the simply natural. We all preach it, from Wordsworth down, and we all, from Wordsworth down, don't practice it. Don't I feel it every day in this weary editorial mill of mine, that there are ten thousand people who can write "ideal" things for one who can see, and feel, and reproduce nature and character? Ten thousand, did I say? Nay, ten million. What made Shakespeare so great? Nothing but eyes and—faith in them. The same is true of Thackeray. I see nowhere more often than in authors the truth that men love their opposites. Dickens insists on being tragic and makes shipwreck.

I always thought (forgive me) that the Hebrew parts of "Dred" were a mistake. Do not think me impertinent: I am only honestly anxious that what I consider a very remarkable genius should have faith in itself. Let your moral take care of itself, and remember that an author's writing-desk is something infinitely higher than a pulpit. What I call "care of itself" is shown in that noble passage in the February number about the ladder up to heaven. That is grand preaching and in the right way. I am sure that "The Minister's Wooing" is going to be the best of your products hitherto, and I am sure of it because you show so thorough a mastery of your material, so true a perception of realities, without which the ideality is impossible.

As for "orthodoxy," be at ease. Whatever is well done the world finds orthodox at last, in spite of all the Fakir journals, whose only notion of orthodoxy seems to be the power of standing in one position till you lose all the use of your limbs. If, with your heart and brain, *you* are not orthodox, in Heaven's name, who is? If you mean "Calvinistic," no woman could ever be such, for Calvinism is logic, and no woman worth the name could ever live by syllogisms. Woman charms a higher faculty in us than reason, God be praised, and nothing has delighted me more in your new story than the happy instinct with which you develop this incapacity of the lovers' logic in your female characters. Go on just as you have begun, and make it appear in as many ways as you like,—that, whatever creed may be true, it is *not* true and never will be that man can be saved by machinery. I can speak with some chance of being right, for I confess a strong sympathy with many parts of Calvinistic theology, and, for one thing, believe in hell with all my might, and in the goodness of God for all that.

I have not said anything. What could I say? One might almost as well advise a mother about the child she still bears under her heart, and say, give it these and those qualities, as an author about a work yet in the brain.

Only this will I say, that I am honestly delighted with "The Minister's Wooing;" that reading it has been one of my few editorial pleasures; that no one appreciates your genius more highly than I, or hopes more fervently that you will let yourself go without regard to this, that, or t'other. Don't read any criticisms on your story: believe that you know better than any of us, and be sure that everybody likes it. That I know. There is not, and never was, anybody so competent to write a true New England poem as yourself, and I have no doubt that you are doing it. The native sod sends up the best inspiration to the brain, and you are as sure of immortality as we all are of dying,—if you only go on with entire faith in yourself.

The English literary establishment agreed with Lowell that *The Minister's Wooing* was the best work Mrs. Stowe had yet produced. Dickens, never effusive unless he was being paid for his writing, was gracious enough to write a brief note saying he enjoyed the new book more than anything she had done. Ruskin wrote a long letter, partly admiring, but critical of the way Mrs. Stowe had handled some of her scenes.

One of the most interesting communications from England was a letter from a woman Mrs. Stowe had not met. Marian Evans, herself a writer, would achieve her first major success in 1859 under the name of George Eliot, when her novel *Adam Bede* was published. She was living openly with George Henry Lewes, one of the most brilliant and versatile of English journalists, who was unable to obtain a divorce from his wife. The letter, its enthusiasm unbridled, made a deep impression on Mrs. Stowe, and thereafter the two women corresponded for many years.

In a number of ways, Harriet Beecher Stowe was becoming more tolerant in her attitudes toward others. Just as she had come to recognize good in Catholicism, she now began to accept the friendship of people whose standards were lower than her own. On her first trip to Europe earlier in the decade, she had refused to meet George Sand in Paris. On her third trip, undertaken soon after the publication of *The Minister's Wooing,* she happily spent a great deal of time in the company of George Eliot, for whose personal plight she developed great sympathy. The world was teaching her that morality could not be as sharply defined as Lyman Beecher had indicated to her in her youth.

North and South drifted toward war in the late 1850s with the ominous inevitability of a Greek tragedy, the pace ever accelerating. President Buchanan, later criticized for his failure to stem the tide, worked frantically to find a solution acceptable to both sides, but the sectionalism he sought to .control instead became more intense.

The panic of 1857, the nation's worst economic depression in two decades, made the situation deteriorate rapidly. The United States had been enjoying one of the biggest booms in its history and, as had happened so often in the past, reckless speculation and foolhardy investment caused the pendulum to swing toward recession. The decline in the industrial North was more severe than in the agricultural South, but both sections suffered.

Scapegoats were easy to find. Unemployed Northern workers, hungry and cold in the winter of 1857-58, blamed the slave labor system south of the Mason-Dixon line. For its part, the South was convinced it was being "punished" by the sharp decline in the prices for the cotton and tobacco on which its economic well-being depended. Western farmers, involved in the country's larger economic patterns for the first time, discovered there was no cash market for their crops.

The shouts of extremists on both sides became increasingly shrill in the elections of 1858, drowning the voices of the moderates, and politicians who sought election to either the Senate or House of Representatives found they were certain of winning seats only if they took an uncompromising stand. Tensions swelled and approached the breaking point on October 16, 1859, when the crazed John Brown, already notorious for his bloody exploits in Kansas three years earlier, led a small group of fanatics in a raid on the federal arsenal at Harpers Ferry, Virginia, and issued a call to the slaves to join him in rebellion against their masters. Brown and his followers were subdued and captured by troops under the command of Colonel Robert E. Lee, and his subsequent execution caused tempers to soar even higher. Many in the North regarded Brown as a martyr, while the South believed he was a tool of abolitionist conspirators.

These developments seem to have left Harriet Beecher Stowe strangely untouched. Although she was, through her first novels, partly responsible for the rise of sectionalism, her opposition to slavery was a matter of high principle, and she failed to recognize the problem in day-to-day terms. Nothing in her magazine articles or correspondence indicates an awareness of the rapid approach of civil war. She and her family suffered relatively few hardships during the panic of 1857 and the slow period of recovery that followed it. Her own furious work pace insulated her from the ouside world, and her income, already enormous and still growing, placed a buffer between her and most of her fellow citizens. It would be an exaggeration to say she had lost sympathy for ordinary people, but she was busier than she had ever been and, still grieving over the loss of Henry, had lost touch with the reality of the world around her.

Nothing better illustrates her growing isolation than her decision to make yet another tour of Europe, accompanied by virtually all of her immediate family. Early in August, 1859, about ten weeks before John Brown's raid on Harpers

Ferry, Professor and Mrs. Stowe sailed for Liverpool, accompanied by sixteen-year-old Georgie. Fred left at about the same time on a sailing vessel with a friend, planning to join the family on the Continent, as would the twins, Hattie and Eliza, still at their Paris boarding school. Only the youngest, Charley, remained at home.

Professor Stowe, his wife, and Georgie visited the Duke and Duchess of Sutherland at their estate and then went on to London, where Mrs. Stowe conferred with her publishers. She also had two meetings with Lady Byron, the first of which was unfruitful because her hostess was suffering one of her "frozen fits." At their second meeting, however, the ladies spent an entire afternoon together, and their conversation was intimate. Whether they discussed Lord Byron is unknown. Mrs. Stowe's only reference to the meeting involved a minor incident. She had forgotten her gloves, and Lady Byron insisted on giving her the pair she herself was wearing; Mrs. Stowe treasured the memento for many years. They did not meet again, as Lady Byron died while her friend was on the Continent; from this time on, Mrs. Stowe felt that she was more than ever responsible to the world for the secret entrusted to her.

The travelers went on to Paris, where they stayed for a week, and then to Switzerland, Hattie and Eliza now members of the party. They were joined for part of their tour by John Ruskin, who later wrote, "I traveled with Mrs. Beecher Stowe and her family...losing a great corner of my heart to her little daughter Georgie in a scramble about the Glacier des Boissons; and discussed immovable articles of faith in a serene picnic by the castle of Valangin above Neuchâtel."

In September the professor and Georgie returned home, the former to resume his responsibilities at the Andover Seminary, the latter to go back to school. Mrs. Stowe and the twins went on to Italy for the winter, stopping briefly in Milan, Verona, Genoa, Venice, and Leghorn. Late in the autumn, they reached Florence, where Fred and his friend joined them, and the family settled down for the winter in a rented apartment.

That period was one of the happiest Mrs. Stowe had known. She enjoyed the company of members of the American colony there, becoming particularly fond of the John T. Howard family, Henry Ward's parishioners, who arrived at about the same time. It was through the Howards that Mrs. Stowe met a couple who would become important to her in the future, Mr. and Mrs. James T. Fields of Boston.

Fields became Mrs. Stowe's publisher when his company, Ticknor and Fields, bought out Phillips and Sampson, as well as the *Atlantic*. Mrs. Fields was even closer to the author, acting informally as her literary agent. Charming, intelligent, and beautiful, Mrs. Fields became Harriet Beecher's confidante, a relationship that was maintained for many years.

Leading literary figures of the period were entertained often at the home of the Fieldses in Boston, and it was there that Mrs. Stowe later solidified her friendships with Nathaniel Hawthorne, James Russell Lowell, John Greenleaf Whittier, Oliver Wendell Holmes, and the woman who became her literary disciple, Sarah Orne Jewett. Mrs. Fields was instrumental, too, in furthering Mrs. Stowe's friendship with George Eliot, and after Mrs. Stowe's death edited and published her correspondence.

Mrs. Fields also helped to smooth her friend's path socially and acted as her defender. Mrs. Stowe, who could relax in the company of people with whom she felt at ease, regardless of their eminence, was still painfully shy on formal occasions, which caused her to behave in a manner some people regarded as eccentric. At a party given in her honor, for example, she was nowhere to be found until Mrs. Fields discovered her in the library, where she was browsing through her host's books, and had to coax her into rejoining the group that came to pay her tribute.

She encountered no such difficulties in Florence, however, opening her doors on Wednesday evenings to friends with whom she chatted by the hour. Her guests were diverse, and included the English novelist Anthony Trollope, as brilliant a conversationalist as he was a writer, and his charming wife, Rose. He and Mrs. Stowe would appear to have little in common other than their vocation, but Trollope was a religious man, whose faith was rooted in the Anglican church, and he and his hostess found common ground in theology.

An even more surprising friendship was that which Mrs. Stowe struck up with Charlotte Cushman, the leading American dramatic actress of the period, who had created a sensation with her Shakespearean portraits on the London stage. Mrs. Stowe's aversion to the theater had not lessened, but she made an exception in the case of Miss Cushman, who, it was said, was incapable of walking quietly into a room. These two women, so opposite in their temperaments and tastes, thoroughly enjoyed each other's company, and their friendship lasted for many years. Mrs. Stowe saw no inconsistency in her attitude.

Another of her visitors was Robert Browning; because his invalid wife could not accompany him, she frequently visited them at home, strengthening the bonds of friendship formed on her previous visit to Florence. One of their ties was a shared growing interest in spiritualism.

Professor Stowe was convinced that the spirit of his drowned son frequently visited him at night, when he sometimes heard a guitar playing, too. When separated from his wife he wrote her in detail about these nocturnal events, sparking her interest in spiritualism. She was sufficiently struck by his experiences to comment, in one letter written from Florence, that she thought it was his first wife, Eliza, rather than Henry who played the guitar for him. Elizabeth Barrettt Browning had also suffered a loss. Her father, with whom she had never been reconciled after her marriage, had died recently, and she desperately sought the solace of communication with him. She and Mrs. Stowe, separately and together, utilized the services of a medium known to posterity only as "Mrs. E. of Boston."

Despite a multitude of differences, all Christian churches of the period were united in their firm denunciation of spiritualism, which was enjoying a great international vogue. How Mrs. Stowe reconciled her new interest with her faith is best revealed in excerpts from a letter she wrote her husband on January 16, 1860, from Florence.

Without doubt [Mrs. E.] is what the spiritualists would regard as a very powerful medium, but being a very earnest Christian, and afraid of getting led astray, she has kept carefully aloof from all circles and things of that nature. She came and opened her mind to me in the first place, to ask my advice as to what she had better do; relating experiences very similar to many of yours.

My advice was substantially to try the spirits whether they were of God,—to keep close to the Bible and prayer, and then accept whatever came. But I have found that when I am with her I receive very strong impressions from the spiritual world, so that I feel often sustained and comforted, as if I had been near to my Henry and other departed friends. This has been at times so strong as greatly to soothe and support me. I told her your experiences, in which she was greatly interested. She said it was so rare to hear of Christian and reliable people with such peculiarities. . . .

I have been reading lately a curious work from an old German in Paris who has been making experiments in spirit-writing. He purports to describe a series of meetings held in the presence of fifty witnesses, whose names he gives, in which writing has come on paper, without the apparition of hands or any pen or pencil, from various historical people.

He seems a devout believer in inspiration, and the book is curious for its mixture of all the phenomena, Pagan and Christian, going over Hindoo, Chinese, Greek, and Italian literatures for examples, and then bringing similar ones from the Bible.

One thing I am convinced of,—that spiritualism is a reaction from the intense materialism of the present age. Luther, when he recognized a personal devil, was much nearer right. We ought to enter fully, at least, into the spiritualism of the Bible. Circles and spiritual jugglery I regard as the lying signs and wonders, with all deceivableness of unrighteousness; but there is a real scriptural spiritualism which has fallen into disuse, and must be revived, and there are, doubtless, people who, from some constitutional formation, can more readily receive the impressions of the surrounding spiritual world. Such were apostles, prophets, and workers of miracles.

This cannot be regarded as Mrs. Stowe's lifelong opinion. Ultimately she changed her mind, becoming more conservative again, and many years later, in a letter to her children, she made her views clear.

Each friend takes away a portion of ourselves ... and again and again, with involuntary yearning, we turn to the stone at the door of the sepulchre. We lean against the cold, silent marble, but there is no answer. ... There are those who would have us think that in *our* day this doom is reversed. ... Ah, *were* it true! ... But for us the stone must be rolled away by an *unquestionable* angel. ... No such angel have we seen. ... And when we look at what is offered to us, ah! who that has friends in heaven could wish them to return in such wise? ... to juggle and rap and squeak and perform mountebank tricks with tables and chairs. ... We have read with some attention weary pages of spiritual communication purporting to come from Bacon, Swedenborg and others. ... If the future life is as weary, stale, flat, and unprofitable as we might infer from these readings, one would have reason to deplore an immortality from which no suicide could give an outlet. ... Is there, then, no satisfaction for this craving of the soul? There is one who says, "I am He that liveth and was dead, and behold I am alive for evermore!" ... He is the true bond of union between the spirit world and our souls; and one blest hour of prayer, when we draw near to Him and feel the breadth, and length, and height of that love of His that passeth knowledge, is better than all those incoherent, vain, dreamy glimpses with which longing hearts are cheated.

Far more important than the discussions of spiritualism that took place under the roof of Robert and Elizabeth Barrett Browning were Mrs. Stowe's meetings there with the Reverend Charles Henry Manning. Father Manning, a recently ordained Roman Catholic priest, made a serious and sustained effort to convert Mrs. Stowe and almost succeeded, but the attitudes instilled in her childhood by Lyman Beecher caused her to hold back. Out of her talks with Father Manning came a new book, *Agnes of Sorrento.* For all practical purposes, her work on *The Pearl of Orr's Island* was complete, and she began to develop the new novel in the spring of 1860 as an intellectual exercise.

Having left Florence with her children, Mr. and Mrs. Fields, and Mr. and Mrs. Howard late in the winter of 1860, Mrs. Stowe went south, making Rome her headquarters and going off on brief sightseeing trips to other cities. By her own admission, she began to weave the tale one morning in Salerno when she and her friends were forced by a rainstorm to spend the entire day sitting beside an inn hearth.

Agnes was conceived as an inquiry into religion in the time of Savonarola, and Mrs. Stowe convinced herself that her characters were Italian, although they closely resembled the New Englanders of *The Minister's Wooing.* The book is marred by one of her more melodramatic plots, almost unbelievable romance, and thick layers of sentiment and well might have been ignored by serious contemporary critics had it been written by anyone other than Harriet Beecher Stowe. It is worthy of modern attention only because it contains a clear exposition of Mrs. Stowe's changed attitude toward Catholicism, which was the result of her greater knowledge of the religion. Her former prejudices have vanished, and she displays an impressively enlightened understanding. When she condemns the Italian peasants of an earlier century for accepting God out of fear, she condemns the superstitious of her own day, whether Protestant or Catholic. To an extent, her Savonarola, the radical preacher who demanded repentance of the Florentines, reflects Lyman Beecher, who utilized man's faith in God to achieve urgently needed reforms in his own world.

Mrs. Stowe's study of various Catholic institutions was remarkably equitable. She acceded that the confessional might be used by the greedy, the powerful, and the lust-ridden to rid themselves of their guilt while continuing to break God's laws and man's, but it performed a vital service in helping the weak become stronger and clarifying the minds and purifying the spirits of the confused. Similarly, the monastery or convent might be used as a hiding place by the lawless, but it provided a spiritual and intellectual refuge for the man of peace and a physical refuge for the helpless woman who had no other place to turn in a savage age when she had few defenders. More than all else, perhaps, the monastery was an incubator where the artist could keep alive the divine spark that was all but extinguished elsewhere.

The most emphatic exposition of her new attitude toward Catholicism can be found in the following excerpt from *Agnes:*

> We can see in the hymns of Savonarola how perfect might be the love and veneration for departed saints without lapsing into idolatry, and with what an atmosphere of warmth and glory the belief in the unity of the Church visible and invisible, could inspire an elevated soul.... To believe in an infinite struggle of intercession which bound all to an interceding Redeemer, so that there was no want or woe of human life that had not somewhere its never-ceasing prayer before the throne of Eternal Love, was far more consoling than the intense individualism of modern philosophy which places the burden upon every soul in its life-battle—scarce even giving it a God to lean upon.

Mrs. Stowe had discovered, perhaps with some surprise, that the doctrines of Catholicism were similar to the Episcopal doctrines she had learned as a child when visiting her grandmother. In fact, the Episcopal creed, which was identical with the Catholic, had been the first she had memorized as a little girl. It was a natural progression, in 1862, when she replied to her daughter Hattie's request to join the Episcopal church, "I not only consent to your joining the Episcopal Church as you have often expressed the desire to do but I desire it so much that I will remove any obstructs in your way. I have applied for a seat in the church in town and I will sometimes go with you—always to sacrament because I find that service is more beneficial than ours.''

Mrs. Stowe privately regarded Episcopalian sermons as dull, and, when attending Anglican services in England, she was irritated by the absence of logical progression in subject matter that she had been taught by her father and brother to regard as essential to a good sermon. By 1864 even these objections fell away, largely because of her growing affinity for the Episcopalian liturgy, and in that year, after moving to Hartford, she completed a religious cycle by giving up the faith of her father and accepting that of her mother, joining the Episcopal church.

14

In April, 1860, Nathaniel Hawthorne and his wife joined Mr. and Mrs. Fields and Mrs. Stowe in Italy, and there was much talk about New England, particularly as the Hawthornes and the Fieldses were planning to return home the following month. Mrs. Stowe had planned to remain in Europe until the end of the summer, but all at once she was overwhelmed by homesickness for her husband, little Charley, and Georgie, so she sailed with her friends and children in May. She made good use of her time on board ship by putting the finishing touches on *The Pearl of Orr's Island* and actively outlining *Agnes of Sorrento*. The twins and Fred saw her only at meals, and she confined her visits with her friends to the evenings.

The whole family was happily reunited in Andover, and Mrs. Stowe plunged into work with the vigor she always displayed after a long holiday. But the outside world intruded as never before, making concentration difficult, and she had to rely on her reserves of will power in order to prepare her books for publication.

The critical presidential election of 1860 was approaching and the future of the United States depended upon the outcome. There were four candidates, and at best the situation was confused. The moderate Senator Stephen A. Douglas of Illinois had been nominated by the Democrats, but the Southern members of the party, advocating the extension of slavery to all territories, broke away and named John C. Breckinridge of Kentucky as their candidate. The Constitutional Union Party, made up principally of Southern moderates striving to preserve the nation, nominated John Bell of Tennessee. The candidate of the new Republican party was Abraham Lincoln of Illinois, who was the center of controversy.

Virtually unknown in the East until February, 1860, when he made an uncompromising antislavery speech in New York, Lincoln took his stand on the premise established by Andrew Jackson, that the preservation of the nation was the first consideration of any President. The South warned it would secede if Lincoln should be elected, and it was obvious this was no idle threat.

Secession was unthinkable to many in the North because the establishment of a new nation in the South would mean that approximately four million slaves would be condemned to continued bondage. Fascinated by publishing since he was an editor in Cincinnati as a young man, Henry Ward Beecher now had an interest in the *Independent* and asked his sister to contribute articles in support of Lincoln. She could not write anything in time for pre-election publication so soon after her return from Europe, but she promised she would help as soon as she could.

The nation voted on November 6, 1860, and within two days enough ballots had been counted to make plain a trend that was soon confirmed: Lincoln had won handily, with 1.8 million votes, about five hundred thousand more than his nearest opponent, Douglas. On December 20, South Carolina became the first state to secede. It was followed in the next month by Mississippi, Florida, Alabama, Georgia, and Louisiana. In February a new nation, the Confederate

States of America, came into being, and was joined by Texas, the seventh of eleven states to secede.

As early as January 9, it became evident that war was inevitable: The *Star of the West,* an unarmed federal supply ship sent by outgoing President Buchanan to Fort Sumter, South Carolina, with provisions, was fired on in Charleston harbor by South Carolina state batteries. Lincoln was inaugurated on March 4, the same day that the Confederate Convention, meeting at Montgomery, Alabama, chose a design for its new flag. The Civil War formally began on April 12, 1861, when Confederate forces fired on Fort Sumter after its commander refused to surrender.

Wendell Phillips and newspaper editor Horace Greeley rejoiced with the abolitionists that the South had broken away; John Greenleaf Whittier wrote a poem that said, in effect, good riddance. President Lincoln, seeking the restoration and preservation of the Union, did not agree.

The Beecher brothers—and their author sister—took their stand with Lincoln, but were less concerned about the state of the Union than the fate of the Southern slaves. Mrs. Stowe put aside her novels to write three impassioned articles for the *Independent,* calling them "The Church and the Slave Trade," "What God Hath Wrought," and "The President's Message." These highly emotional appeals concentrated almost exclusively on the question of slavery; legal, political, and economic matters, not to mention the Constitutional question of whether a state had the right to secede, were scarcely touched on. In her own way, Mrs. Stowe offered Lincoln her full support but made it plain in her personal correspondence that she would withdraw it if he should equivocate on the slavery issue at any time.

The young men of the Beecher family did not hesitate to do their part in the war their elders had helped precipitate. Less than twenty-four hours after the attack on Fort Sumter, James Beecher, Mrs. Stowe's half brother, obtained a commission and was assigned to the force guarding Washington, D.C., which was in danger of falling into Confederate hands.

He was joined by several of his nephews, the first to enlist being Mrs. Stowe's son Fred, who had just celebrated his twenty-first birthday. Tall, slender, and serious, sometimes melancholy, and always afraid he could not live up to the luster of his name, Frederick Stowe had struggled since childhood to overcome the handicaps of a delicate constitution. As he departed, he expressed the fear that "the son of Harriet Beecher Stowe might die a coward's death." That thought continued to haunt him, even though he subsequently distinguished himself in action and, within a year and a half, won a battlefield commission as a lieutenant.

Fred was ever present in the thoughts of his parents, as their correspondence with others in the family indicates, and both wrote to him regularly. Unfortunately, Mrs. Stowe kept no copies of her letters to him, and, as a soldier in the field had no storage facilities available, her communications have not survived.

Meanwhile, there were contractual obligations to be fulfilled, and two of Mrs. Stowe's books were published at the same time. The second part of *The Pearl of Orr's Island* appeared at intervals in serial form in the *Independent* between April, 1861, and April, 1862, the entire work being printed in book form immediately thereafter by Ticknor and Fields. *Agnes of Sorrento* enjoyed the unusual distinction of being serialized in two publications, the *Atlantic Monthly* and *Cornhill Magazine,* beginning in May, 1861, and ending in May, 1862. Ticknor and Fields brought it out as a book in June, 1862. Both books enjoyed the sales, both at home and abroad, to which Harriet Beecher Stowe had become accustomed. From the outset, critics recognized *Agnes* as a minor work, but that knowledge in no way impeded its popularity, and it sold almost four hundred thousand copies in the United States alone. Reviewers at home and in Great Britain were quick to hail *The Pearl of Orr's Island* as a superior effort. The public concurred, and the book continued to sell at a brisk clip for more than two decades; in all, more than seven hundred thousand copies were sold in the United States.

It was hailed by Whittier, Hawthorne, and Lowell, and

Sarah Orne Jewett, writing many years later, called it a classic. Modern students of American literature agree that in *The Pearl* Mrs. Stowe excelled herself.

Mrs. Stowe's faithful readers found few surprises in the book. Her setting was rural Maine, her characters were composites of people she had known there, combined with the basic types who were always present in her imagination, and once again she was concerned with religion, this time the good and the bad to be found in primitive Calvinism.

Her heroine, Mara, is one of her tranquil young ladies whose rocklike faith in God gives her a serenity nothing can shake. In many ways, she is similar to all of Mrs. Stowe's other heroines, and, like little Eva in *Uncle Tom's Cabin*, she dies of consumption. Before she departs from the world, however, she succeeds in reforming the hero of the book, Moses, one of Mrs. Stowe's devil-may-care young men, whose feet are eventually turned to the path of righteousness.

From time to time, Mara veers perilously close to caricature, as, for example, when she is described by another character as one who has "got the real New-Jerusalem look... like them in the Revelations that wears the fine linen, clean and white." A far superior creation, as are relatively minor female characters found in a number of Mrs. Stowe's other novels, is Sally Kittredge. Fond of pretty clothes and always quick to speak her own mind, Sally is not above flirting with young men, although harmlessly, to be sure. She never exceeds the bounds of good taste, as Mrs. Stowe saw them, and like so many of the author's other secondary heroines she becomes a responsible Christian matron after she is married.

The Pearl is noteworthy because it reflects the influence of Shakespeare on Mrs. Stowe. Although she occasionally referred to *Macbeth* as her favorite play, she admitted that *The Tempest* had fascinated her since she first read it as a child, and she made her feelings plain when she called one chapter of *The Pearl* "The Enchanted Island."

She displays little interest in comparative religion in the book, but repeatedly looks back to the early Puritan societies as the ideal. They were "democratic, simple, solemn and religious, yet full of wholesome thrift and prosperity." Households had calmness and dignity, but family feelings and loyalties were intense. Ministers were men of purity and abiding faith in God and communicated their beliefs to their congregations in a manner that produced a whole, harmonious community. Yet the minister held no special place in a town because of his position. Like all others, he was an ordinary citizen, and if people accepted what he taught it was because he was endowed with the inner authority to preach the Word; people accepted it because they recognized it as the truth. Mrs. Stowe recognized no conflict here, none of the materialism that, as she saw it, debased and degraded religion in her own world.

Viewed strictly as a novel, *The Pearl* is hackneyed, and as a treatise on faith it is banal. But it gripped its readers and, more than a century after its initial publication, it continues to exude considerable charm. Its strength, perhaps more evident than in any of Mrs. Stowe's other books, is the explicit, homely detail with which she delineates day-to-day living in rural Maine.

In this sense *The Pearl* is realistic, and it was influential in laying the foundations for the realism in fiction by others that followed. Mrs. Stowe presented a portrait of the life she knew so well because she herself had struggled to create a home in near-primitive surroundings. Walking a tightrope, she refrained from glorifying the way of life that was universal in early America, but at the same time she managed to tint it with romanticism, encouraging her readers to forget the hardships and to yearn for a healthy, rugged, and wholesome society.

The Pearl of Orr's Island, begun when Mrs. Stowe lived in Maine, and intermittently in preparation ever since she completed the writing of *Uncle Tom's Cabin,* was published at precisely the time when it would most appeal to her reading public. Deeply disturbed by the war that had torn the United States apart, the bloodiest and most costly in the nation's history, Northerners instinctively longed for simple earlier values, for the uncomplicated "good life" they imagined their American ancestors had led. *The Pearl* presented the elements that had been the building blocks of a strong and wealthy country now being threatened with dissolution. *The Pearl* reflected a legacy in which Americans could take pride. Mrs. Stowe was told that Lincoln read and enjoyed the book, but the report may have been in error. It is unlikely that the beleaguered President had time to read fiction.

After Mrs. Stowe completed *The Pearl of Orr's Island* and *Agnes of Sorrento,* at about the time hostilities broke out, she was able to devote her attention to the war and its ramifications. In June she made a business trip to New York, staying with Henry Ward and his family in Brooklyn, and spent a day visiting Frederick at a military training camp in New Jersey. She made it her business to meet his regimental chaplain, and after assuring herself the latter was a good Christian she felt a trifle more relaxed. Her son was in safe hands.

One development outraged and bewildered Mrs. Stowe: The government of Great Britain, led by Lord Palmerston and supported by the majority of public opinion, favored the cause of the Confederacy. In her mind, the issue was simple: One stood for or against slavery. Never did she demonstrate an understanding of the complex economic and social issues that led the British to adopt their position. Great Britain's mills comprised its leading industry, and its prosperity depended on the ability to obtain an uninterrupted supply of Confederate cotton. Fortunately, enough was stored in warehouses at the beginning of the war to last the better part of a year, which gave the country freedom to maneuver.

Shipping interests joined forces with mill owners, and their reasons were basic, too. The rapid growth of the American merchant marine had hurt the British, but the war badly disrupted Northern trade, and British commercial shipping benefited accordingly.

Subtle influences were also at work, tipping the scales, in the British Isles. The aristocrats who ruled Britain for many years long had felt antipathetic toward the experiment in popular democracy being conducted by former colonies and felt a kinship with the landed gentry of the South. The London *Times* expressed the sentiments of the upper class when it said, "The contest is really for empire on the side of the North and for independence on that of the South."

Public opinion in Britain was far from unanimous, however. The friends of the Union in Parliament were in a minority, but from the first appeared strong enough to prevent the government from recognizing the Confederacy. Nature temporarily came to the aid of the North, too: A drought in Britain caused crop failures there in 1860, 1861, and 1862 that made it dependent on the wheat, barley, corn, and oats of the Union.

Influential voices were raised in favor of the Confederacy. Charles Dickens wrote persuasively on behalf of the South, and so did the Scotch essayist and historian Thomas Carlyle. The less influential Alfred Tennyson was a Northern adherent, as was Charles Darwin.

The stakes for the combatants in the ultimate position taken by Great Britain were enormous, and both knew it. France had already indicated it would take no initiative, Napoleon III hinting he would follow London's lead. If pro-Southern opinion in Britain became strong enough, Palmerston's government might be persuaded to extend official recognition to the Confederacy. This would force the Union to declare war, and the South would no longer stand alone but would be joined by two powerful allies, Britain and France.

Henry Ward Beecher was a worldly man, well able to grasp the complexities of power politics, and he explained the situation to his sister during her June, 1861, visit to Brooklyn. Harriet Beecher Stowe returned to her Massachusetts home with a mission. Possibly *Uncle Tom's Cabin* had sold fewer copies in Britain than *Oliver Twist* or *David Copperfield*, although she doubted it, and she regarded herself as a match for Dickens. He had left his wife, then taken a young actress as his mistress, and she felt certain the women of Great Britain would reject his position in favor of her own highly moral one.

Uppermost in Mrs. Stowe's mind was the response of

the British of all classes when she made her antislavery tour
of Scotland and England in 1853, following the publication of
Uncle Tom's Cabin. There was a huge reservoir of pro-
freedom, pro-Northern sentiment in the British Isles and
Empire, but it had to be tapped. For proof of its existence
she needed to look no farther than her own library, where
the embossed twenty-six-volume set of the "Affectionate
and Christian Address from the Women of Great Britain"
reposed. She knew without looking at the signatures that it
had been signed by 562,448 women opposed to slavery.

Those same women, their ranks augmented by others,
could turn the tide of British sentiment in favor of the Union.
At no previous time had it crossed her mind to reply to the
"Address," but now it was her God-inspired duty to do so.
No American name was better known in Britain than her
own, and, not only did people automatically associate her
with the antislavery cause, but they knew she had always
been moderate, compassionate, and Christian in her outlook.

In preparing the document, she had to be more cautious
than she had ever been in writing her novels and articles.
Every word mattered, every phrase would be subjected to
critical scrutiny by friends and scorned by enemies.

First, and most important, she had to be sure of the position taken on slavery by the United States Government.
She approved of President Lincoln but sometimes felt uneasy
when she realized that since the outbreak of the war he had said
very little on the subject of slavery.

On September 23, 1862, Lincoln issued a proclamation
that eased her mind somewhat. The slaves of all states in rebellion would be free unless those states gave up the fight
and returned to the Union within ninety days. The proclamation was intended as a form of political pressure, and the
President knew better than anyone that it would have no
practical effect on the Confederacy. That, however, was of no
consequence to Mrs. Stowe. He had taken a step in the right
direction, and all she needed to do was to meet him herself
so she could form an estimate of his character.

Meanwhile, preparing a draft of her "Reply to the

Address," she studied letters she had received from various English friends. In March, 1861, on the eve of the war, Elizabeth Barrett Browning had touched on the subject in a long letter largely devoted to other matters:

> Now let me be ashamed of this egotism, together with the rest of the weakness obtruded on you here, when I should rather have congratulated you, my dear friend, on the crisis you are passing through in America. If the North is found noble enough to stand fast on the moral question, whatever the loss or diminution of territory, God and just men will see you greater and more glorious as a nation.
>
> I had much anxiety for you after the Seward and Adams speeches, but the danger seems averted by that fine madness of the South which seems judicial. The tariff movement we should regret deeply (and do, some of us), only I am told it was wanted in order to persuade those who were less accessible to moral argument. It's eking out the holy water with ditch water. If the Devil flees before it, even so, let us be content. How you must feel, *you* who have done so much to set this accursed slavery in the glare of the world, convicting it of hideousness! They should raise a statue to you in America and elsewhere.

Mrs. Browning's attitude was the core of Mrs. Stowe's dilemma. The English poet loathed slavery, of course, but Mrs. Stowe felt she erred in speaking of the moral victory the North was enjoying. There could be no victory, moral or otherwise, until the four million wretched slaves in the South were set free.

Mrs. Stowe kept on her desk, plainly visible at all times, an article from Horace Greeley's *New York Tribune* that Henry Ward had sent her. It warned, all too clearly, that unless the South was compelled to accept total emancipation, the freed slaves of the Confederacy, perhaps as many as five hundred thousand of them, would be forced into bondage again. The women of Great Britain had to be made to understand that full emancipation provided the only solution to the world's most compelling problem.

Early in November, 1862, Mrs. Stowe received an invitation to a Thanksgiving dinner being held in Washington, D.C., for a thousand former slaves. She accepted by return mail, at the same time initiating the arrangements for a meeting with the President. Apparently it did not cross her mind that Lincoln might be too busy to see her.

She arrived in Washington the Saturday before Thanksgiving, hoping to spend Sunday with Fred, now Lieutenant Frederick Stowe, whose regiment was stationed in nearby Maryland. Military red tape delayed the meeting, a particularly annoying turn of events, as Charley was accompanying his mother in the hope of seeing his big brother in uniform. When Harriet Beecher Stowe made up her mind to do something, however, not even the United States Army could stand in her way.

She had no military passes, but she and Charley nevertheless boarded the Maryland train and reached their destination without interference. After renting rooms at the local inn, Mrs. Stowe hired a carriage to take her to the encampment. Men on duty in the field were allowed no visitors, but she brushed aside the regimental commander and went straight to the brigade commander. Mrs. Beecher Stowe, author of *Uncle Tom's Cabin,* wanted to see her son: Permission granted. Mrs. Stowe wanted to take her son back to the nearby town to have dinner with her and spend the night: Permission granted. She also wanted him given a week's leave to accompany her to Washington, where she had an appointment with the President the day after Thanksgiving. Would she put that request in writing? She would and did immediately, in what she described to her husband as a "pathetic" letter.

Fred, she told Professor Stowe, was "looking very well, has grown in thickness, and is as loving and affectionate as a boy can be." She seems to have been blinded by a mother's love. Lieutenant Stowe, who had already met the enemy in combat five times, was no longer a boy, but a man. In spite of the courage and efficiency he had shown in the field, sufficient to win him a commission without the exertion of parental influence, he was still haunted by the fear that he would be shown up in battle as a coward. That dread, combined with the memories of slaughter he carried with him, were affecting him so severely that, like many other young officers inadequately trained for war, he drank quantities of whiskey whenever he had the opportunity.

At the inn that night, Mrs. Stowe was paid a call by her son's division commander, Major General Buckingham, and displayed her knowledge of military affairs in her chat with him. She remarked to her husband, "General B.... was the officer deputed to carry the order to General McClellan relieving him of command of the army. He carried it to him in his tent about twelve o'clock at night. Burnside was there. McClellan said it was very unexpected, but immediately turned over the command. I said I thought he ought to have expected it after having so disregarded the President's order. General B. smiled and said he supposed McClellan had done that so often before that he had no idea any notice would be taken of it this time."

In the course of the conversation, Mrs. Stowe, who knew so many people in high places that a mere major general failed to impress her, repeated her request for a one-week leave for Frederick. Request denied. Buckingham, himself a father as well as a general officer, explained that the effect on his division's morale would be harmful if he showed favoritism. Mrs. Stowe accepted the decision philosophically, writing her husband, "we had had to content ourselves with what we could have."

Before General Buckingham departed, however, Mrs. Stowe deeply embarrassed her son. At dinner he had told her he was tired of serving in the infantry because it entailed so much garrison duty and wished he could be transferred to the cavalry, with the prospect of constant action. He had assumed his conversation with his mother was confidential, but apparently he did not know her as well as he thought. To his horror, Mrs. Stowe repeated his request and the reasons for it to his commander. General Buckingham grinned but made no comment as he took his leave. Less than a month later,

Frederick Stowe was transferred to the cavalry, where he soon won another promotion, thanks to his valor in combat, to the rank of captain.

Mrs. Stowe was deeply impressed by the dinner for the former slaves, and for the rest of her life remembered they were "Christians who sang hymns." Never had her heart been so full of gratitude to God, she wrote, and never had she been so determined to win freedom for all slaves.

The following day she and Charley went to the White House, accompanied by Representative Henry Wilson of Massachusetts, her congressman, who happened to be chairman of the House Committee on Military Affairs. At no time thereafter did she make any mention of the meeting in her correspondence or elsewhere, and it is impossible to guess what she thought of Abraham Lincoln. There was no particular reason why she should have recorded her views; although she was acquainted with scores of renowned men and women, only infrequently did she note her reactions to them. Neither the President nor Congressman Wilson remarked on the meeting, either, so posterity's only record comes from the recollected experience of a twelve-year-old boy.

Writing many years later, Charles Stowe remembered that President Lincoln was sitting with his feet propped on the mantel before an open fire when his visitors came into his study. He put aside the papers he was reading and clumsily hauled himself to his feet. He liked an open fire, he said. So did her family, Mrs. Stowe replied. That took care of the amenities. Charles Stowe recalled with a trace of condescension that Lincoln said "to home" instead of "at home." He is the source of the famous remark—true or the product of his imagination—attributed to Lincoln, "So this is the little lady who made this big war."

Without question, the President and Mrs. Stowe must have discussed his Preliminary Emancipation Proclamation, due to take effect on January 1, 1863, and his immediate plans. It was no secret that he intended to issue a final and full Emancipation Proclamation on that date, as "a necessary war measure," setting free all slaves in the states still in rebellion and inviting them to join the armed forces of the Union. The proclamation would contain no mention of slavery in states loyal to the Union, where it already existed, like Missouri, or in portions of Tennessee, Virginia, and Louisiana occupied by Northern troops.

Lincoln, a master politician, probably explained his strategy to her. He had no desire to turn the border states against the Union and consequently was deliberately omitting them from his final Emancipation Proclamation. But the net effect of his order would be to doom the institution of slavery everywhere. In fact, he had already received private assurances that the legislatures of Kentucky, Tennessee, Missouri, Maryland, Delaware, and West Virginia (which would be granted statehood in 1863), would quickly fall into line. Once slavery was made illegal in the heartland of the South, it could not survive in the border states, but they were to be given the opportunity to rid themselves of it in the manner best suiting their dignity.

If any state proved lax, the President may have said, he would intervene and abolish slavery by executive order. In any event, sentiment in favor of a Constitutional amendment permanently abolishing slavery everywhere in the United States was developing rapidly and not only would have his unqualified support but was certain to become law within the next twelve or eighteen months.

Mrs. Stowe's actions illuminate her reaction to President Lincoln as well anything she may have said. When the meeting ended, she returned to her Washington hotel suite with Charley, and after supper spent the whole night at the desk in the parlor, revising and polishing her "Reply to an Address from the Women of Great Britain." Her last doubts about Lincoln must have vanished; she accepted his word and became his ardent supporter and defender.

The following morning, she dated her communication, "Washington, November 27, 1862," and mailed it to the *Atlantic Monthly*, where it was eagerly awaited. The "Reply," published in January, 1863, on the heels of the final Emancipation Proclamation, created a sensation in the United

States as well as in Great Britain. Its effect was intensified when, later in the year, Henry Ward Beecher made an extensive speaking tour of the British Isles and frequently quoted from his sister's work.

The British Government was placed in an exceptionally uncomfortable position. An attempt might have been made to ignore or discount the Emancipation Proclamation, but the barrage of publicity incited by Mrs. Stowe and her brother made this impossible. President Lincoln later attributed Britain's failure to extend diplomatic recognition to the Confederacy to three factors: *Uncle Tom's Cabin,* Mrs. Stowe's "Reply," and the Reverend Henry Ward Beecher's British tour. The most distinguished of his Confederate opponents, General Robert E. Lee, was in complete agreement with his assessment. And Oliver Wendell Holmes wrote that the "Reply" was the equivalent of a decisive Union victory.

As always, Mrs. Stowe had pulled no punches. The "Reply" was addressed by name to twenty-two of Britain's most prominent ladies, among them four duchesses, three countesses, Lady Palmerston, and the wife of the dean of St. Paul's Cathedral. Saluting them as "sisters," she first quoted in full their "Address." Then, in about five thousand words, she issued a sharp rebuke to the more than half a million women who had failed to raise their voices in protest when their government dared to contemplate recognition of the Confederacy.

> Your address reached us just as a great moral conflict was coming to its intensest point. The agitation kept up by the anti-slavery portion of America, by England, and by the general sentiment of humanity in Europe, had made the situation of the slaveholding aristocracy intolerable. As one of them at the time expressed it, they felt themselves under the ban of the civilized world. Two courses only were open to them: to abandon slave institutions, the sources of their wealth and political power, or to answer them with such an overwhelming national force as to compel the assent and respect of mankind. They chose the latter....

It has been often and earnestly asserted that slavery had nothing to do with this conflict; that it was a mere struggle for power; that the only object was to restore the Union as it was, with all its abuses. It is to be admitted that expressions have proceeded from the national administration which naturally gave rise to misapprehension, and therefore we beg to speak to you more fully on this subject.

And first the declaration of the Confederate States themselves is proof enough that, whatever may be declared on the other side, the maintenance of slavery is regarded by them as the vital object of their movement....

The United States has in its highest official capacity taken distinct anti-slavery ground, and presented to the country a plan of peaceable emancipation with suitable compensation. This noble-spirited and generous offer has been urged on the slaveholding States by the chief executive with earnestness and sincerity.... Lastly, the great decisive measure of the war has appeared,—the President's Proclamation of Emancipation.

This also has been much misunderstood and misrepresented in England. It has been said to mean virtually this: Be loyal and you shall keep your slaves; rebel and they shall be free.... The President's Proclamation simply means this: Come in and emancipate peaceably with compensation; stay out and I will emancipate, nor will I protect you from the consequences.

Will our sisters in England feel no heartbeat at that event? Is it not one of the predicted voices of the latter day, saying under the whole Heavens, "It is done; the kingdoms of this world are become the kingdoms of our Lord and of His Christ"?

And now, sisters of England, in this solemn, expectant hour, let us speak to you of one thing which fills our hearts with pain and solicitude. It is an unaccountable fact, and one which we entreat you seriously to ponder, that the party which has brought the cause of freedom thus far on its way, during the past eventful year, has found little or no support in England. Sadder than this, this party which makes slavery the chief corner-stone of its edifice finds in England its strongest defenders.

Harriet Beecher Stowe

The voices that have spoken for us who contend for liberty have been few and scattering. God forbid that we should forget those few noble voices, so sadly exceptional in the general outcry against us! They are, alas! too few to be easily forgotten. False statements have blinded the mind of your community, and turned the most generous sentiments of the British heart against us. The North are fighting for supremacy and the South for independence has been the voice. Independence for what? to do what? To prove the doctrine that all men are *not* equal; to establish the doctrine that the white may enslave the negro!

This very day the writer of this has been present at a solemn religious festival in the national capital, given at the home of a portion of those fugitive slaves who have fled to our lines for protection,—who, under the shadow of our flag, find sympathy and succor. . . . As we were leaving, an aged woman came and lifted up her hands in blessing. "Bressed be de Lord dat brought me to see dis first happy day of my life! Bressed be de Lord!"

In all England is there no Amen?

What! give up the point of emancipation for these four million slaves? Turn our backs on them, and leave them to their fate? What! leave our white brothers to run a career of oppression and robbery that, as sure as there is a God that ruleth in the armies of heaven, will bring down a day of wrath and doom? Remember that wishing success to this slavery-establishing effort is only wishing to the sons and daughters of the South all the curses that God has written against oppression.

Mark our words!

If we succeed, the children of these very men who are now fighting us will rise up to call us blessed. Just as surely as there is a God who governs in the world, so surely all the laws of national prosperity will follow in the train of equity; and if we succeed, we shall have delivered the children's children of our misguided brethren from the wages of sin, which is always and everywhere death.

And now, sisters of England, think it not strange if we bring back the words of your letter, not in bitterness, but in deepest sadness, and lay them down at your door.

We say to you, Sisters, you have spoken well; we have heard you; we have heeded; we have striven in the cause, even unto death. We have sealed our devotion by the desolate hearth and darkened homesteads,—by the blood of sons, husbands, and brothers. In many of our dwellings the very light of our lives has gone out; and yet we accept the life-long darkness as our own part in this great and awful expiation, by which the bonds of wickedness shall be loosed, and abiding peace established on the foundation of righteousness. Sisters, what have *you* done, and what do you mean to do?

We appeal to you as sisters, as wives, as mothers, to raise your voices to your fellow-citizens, and your prayers to God for the removal of this affliction and disgrace from the Christian world.

In behalf of many thousands of American women.

Duty had many faces, Harriet Beecher Stowe had read in her childhood, and even at the age of fifty-one, in 1862, she remembered the quotation, although she could no longer trace its source. First, she believed, came her duty to her husband.

Professor Stowe was scheduled to be retired by the Andover Theological Seminary in the spring of 1863, and his wife made energetic plans for his future. It was unthinkable that a man of his knowledge do nothing, so she proposed he write a book, *The Origin and History of the Books of the Bible*. She would edit the work for him, to the extent that he permitted, and, funds being ample, they would publish it themselves, thereby reaping all the profits. The professor was willing.

He was far less amenable to another of her schemes: They would move to Hartford, the scene of some of her happiest girlhood memories, and not only would they be near her sisters Mary Perkins and Isabella Hooker but they would build a house in a grove of oaks on the Park River, the woods in which she had strolled with Georgiana May. The mere contemplation of the house inspired Mrs. Stowe.

They would build a Gothic great-house, similar to the mansions she had visited in England. It would be three stories high, with a half basement as well, at least eight gables, and a huge double entrance hall. The formal parlor, family sitting room, library, and dining room would be paneled in natural oak taken from the grove, as would her husband's sitting room and her own work chamber, her very first in all the years she had been earning money with her pen. Stables and a carriage house would be placed in the rear, and opposite the main house would stand a two-story conservatory, with an Italian fountain located between the two structures. There would be formal and informal outdoor gardens, too, as well as a vegetable patch of two acres, and a portion of the oak grove would be left in its natural state to preserve the family's privacy.

The professor was aghast. He enjoyed living in the Andover house, and if his wife wanted to become a landowner they could buy the place for a fraction of what the mansion would cost. Besides, he felt such an estate would bankrupt them; while it was true that his wife was earning a substantial living, their funds were not unlimited, and not even a wealthy English nobleman could afford the cost and upkeep of a palace.

Mrs. Stowe ignored his protests, paid no attention to the figures he showed her, and plunged ahead. She would allow nothing to interfere with the realization of a lifelong dream, and she was determined to make the move the very week her husband retired, in the spring of 1863. The professor's retirement took place on schedule, and so did the move into a half-finished house.

Mrs. Stowe had to confer endlessly with architects and building foremen; buy furniture, rugs, drapes, and curtains; hire and train servants; and, above all, keep out of the way of carpenters, painters, plumbers, and masons. When the Stowes arrived, the central staircase was unfinished and the entire family had to use the back stairs; oak paneling had not yet been installed; only one bathroom was operable; and few rooms had doors yet.

The professor added to her burdens. He was constantly underfoot, complaining about the unnecessary expense, and unable to start writing his masterwork because of the confusion. The twins, Eliza and Hattie, did what they could to help their mother, who wanted no assistance, but made it plain they agreed with their father. They were not mollified when Mrs. Stowe reminded them that their suite had its own private sitting room, and she remembered the ingratitude of King Lear's elder daughters.

Charley and a friend, playing a forbidden game of ball on the lawn, broke a large conservatory window before it could be installed, and there was a delay of months before another could be made and delivered. Georgie had a suitor, a clergyman, in the Beecher tradition, and the Reverend Henry Allen, pastor of an Episcopalian church in Stockbridge, Massachusetts, seemed to be continually in and out of the house. One warm afternoon in the late spring, Professor Stowe stole off to a small unoccupied bedroom at the rear of the house so that he could read in peace without being interrupted by workmen. He had just dozed off when the plumbing in the ceiling overhead erupted, subjecting him to a shower of water and plaster.

But Mrs. Stowe had real sorrows and worries on her mind and was not concerned about trifles. In January, 1863, Lyman Beecher had died in Brooklyn at his home, near Henry Ward's parsonage. Ill, bedridden, and increasingly senile, he had rallied in his last moments, and with his children gathered around him he made his farewell with a typical flourish. "I have fought a good fight, I have finished my course," he told them. The good he had done would live after him, for his sons and daughters consecrated themselves anew to complete the work he had started. They mourned his passage, although they rejoiced because his soul was immortal. Feeling her loss, Mrs. Stowe inundated herself in work on the new house.

One anxiety she could not dispel was for Frederick. Twice she and the professor were notified that he had been commended for bravery in action. He commanded a troop of cavalry now and appeared to have developed a relish for danger. Late in June, 1863, the war news became ominous. General Lee and his strongest army used the Shenandoah Valley as a corridor and crossed the Potomac River. A force under General George G. Meade awaited him on the heights of Gettysburg in southern Pennsylvania, and there, beginning on July 1, the worst battle of the war was fought. It lasted for three days before Lee, in a superb feat, managed to extricate his army and retire in good order. More than forty thousand Union and Confederate soldiers were killed, and so many were wounded that newspapers lacked the space to print the casualty lists.

The Stowes, like thousands of other parents, waited in dread to learn what might have happened to their son. The War Department announced that the scene of battle was so confused it might be many days before the dead, wounded, and missing could be identified and notification sent to their families. Mrs. Stowe had friends in the United States Senate and House of Representatives, admirers in the army high command. In her time of trial, however, she would neither seek nor accept privilege. All men were equal in the sight of God, who knew no favorites, she believed, so she and her husband would wait patiently on the Lord.

Almost two weeks after the Battle of Gettysburg ended, Mrs. Stowe received a letter, dated July 11, written by a regimental chaplain.

> Among the thousands of wounded and dying men on this war-scarred field, I have just met with your son, Captain Stowe. If you have not already heard from him, it may cheer your heart to know that he is in the hands of good, kind friends. He was struck by a fragment of a shell, which entered his right ear. He is quiet and cheerful, longs to see some member of his family, and is, above all, anxious that they should hear from him as soon as possible. I assured him I would write at once, and though I am wearied by a week's labor here among scenes of terrible suffering, I know that, to a mother's anxious

heart, even a hasty scrawl about her boy will be more than welcome.

May God bless and sustain you in this troubled time.

Captain Stowe was transferred to a military hospital in New York, where his parents visited him, and in the autumn of 1863, having been diagnosed as unfit for further military duty, he was granted an honorable discharge. He received further treatment from private physicians, first in New York and then in Boston, but they could do nothing for him, and he came to the family's new home in Hartford. The shell fragment had been removed from his head, but he still suffered from blinding headaches, and his mother noticed that his conduct was sometimes inexplicably erratic.

His sisters and young brother knew—as did the professor, in all probability—that Fred was drinking to excess. But the family banded together to keep this fact from his mother. It was inconceivable to them that one reared in a household where temperance was a byword could become "a slave to alcohol," as Eliza put it. Soon Fred's health would improve, his memory of the Gettysburg ordeal would become less intense, and he would recover from his aberration.

He expressed enthusiasm for his mother's suggestion that he study medicine under Dr. Oliver Wendell Holmes, and she saw him off to Boston with high hopes. She displayed silent courage when the truth of his situation was revealed to her: Fred had become a drunkard.

No one gave her a chance to put his condition out of her mind. When he was in Boston, and during his later wanderings, too, strangers seemed to delight in writing to Mrs. Stowe that they had seen her son in an intoxicated condition. She had taken such a firm stand in favor of temperance in her writing, as had her father and brothers from their pulpits, that she appears to have been an irresistible target.

Harriet Beecher Stowe could and did complain at length about fatigue and minor ailments, but, as she had demonstrated when Henry died, her backbone was very firm in a time of real crisis. She made no public reply to the taunting letters about Frederick, referred to them with contempt in her family correspondence, and kept her real worries about her son to herself, discussing the problem with no one but the professor. At no time, either in her letters or elsewhere, did she ever admit that Frederick had a drinking problem. Her position was that he had suffered a severe wound at Gettysburg, which was true, and it had made his conduct somewhat unusual, which was also true. She had never washed her dirty linen in the presence of others, and she did not intend to begin now.

Frederick's mortification was intense. For years he had been afraid that he would be called a coward, and he had performed deeds of valor to disprove his fears. Now, as Charles Stowe wrote many years later, he was crushed by the realization that the son of Harriet Beecher Stowe was a confirmed drunkard, but he was incapable of curing himself. Nineteenth-century medicine knew so little about the disease that physicians could do nothing for him either.

There were other matters on Mrs. Stowe's mind, as well. Throughout the war, she continued to write regularly for the *Atlantic,* the *Independent,* and other magazines, turning out an article every four or five weeks. Her agreement with the *Atlantic* stipulated that she could write for no other publication, as Annie Fields sometimes reminded her in letters from Boston, but she blithely ignored the restriction. For one thing, she found she needed the money.

The professor had been right when he told her the mansion would swallow dollars as fast as she could earn them. A year and a half after they moved in, it was not yet finished, and the construction bills continued to pour in every month. No amount of coal and wood heated the house adequately, a staff of four servants could not keep it clean, and, worst of all, new factories began to move into the area, lowering the value of the property.

Mrs. Stowe refused to admit defeat and wrote still more magazine articles, the majority of them on the theme that the approaching victory of the North would ensure the end of slavery for all time. Two new strains appeared in her work. After the war was won, she wrote, every citizen of the North had a solemn obligation to help the former slaves find profitable employment. And she warned, too, that recriminations against the South would sow the seeds of future discord. Defeat and the end of slavery would be humiliation and punishment enough. "One nation must live in brotherhood," she wrote in the *Atlantic,* and her voice was one of the first raised in favor of compassion toward the Confederacy after it had returned to the Union.

Countless thousands regarded Mrs. Stowe as a living symbol of the ideals for which the North stood. On New Year's Day, 1863, when President Lincoln issued his final Emancipation Proclamation, she and the professor happened to be in Boston, visiting the Fieldses. Her presence there became known, and a huge crowd gathered outside the house and gave her a spontaneous ovation that lasted until she came to an open window and bowed.

Throughout the war she received so much mail that she needed two full-time secretaries to answer it. Several sacks of letters were delivered to her each day by the Hartford post office; as she would have had time for nothing else had she read all of them, she looked only at those called to her special attention.

Her private charities were endless. She devoted time and money to the rehabilitation of "A——," a "fallen woman." She took in an urchin off the streets, clothed and fed him, and was unperturbed when he vanished again the following day. The clothing and a good meal, she said, had better prepared him for his uncertain future.

In the early summer of 1864, Georgie became Mrs. Henry Allen, and the conservatory and garden of the new Stowe house became the scene of the largest and most lavish wedding reception in Hartford history. Those who were envious of Mrs. Stowe—and there were many—claimed she was flaunting her wealth, but her husband believed she was deliberately distracting herself so that she would worry less about Frederick.

Perhaps in part for the same reason, Mrs. Stowe's literary output remained prodigious throughout the decade. Her articles and essays covered a wide variety of subjects, ranging from the patriotic duty of Northerners to buy only domestic manufactured goods to the new types of recreation sought by young people; from the decorating of a house to the growing of camellias in hothouses. But it is also undoubtedly true that her need for money to pay for her Gothic palace and maintain it was enormous; the result was that almost anything and everything that crossed her mind became grist for her mill.

Between 1863 and 1870, she scribbled a total of ten books. She produced a volume of short stories for children, and another of religious poems. She increased her work pace to such an extent that she was able to churn out dozens of articles, many for the *Atlantic,* that were published under the pseudonym of Christopher Crowfield. Many of these pieces appeared in book collections under the titles *House and Home Papers, Little Foxes, Ravages of a Carpet,* and *The Chimney Corner.* Most made light reading and apparently were written with ease.

The work that attracted the most attention during this period was a four-volume series of short biographies called *Men of Our Times,* first published in 1868 and again four years later, after additions and corrections had been made. A number of contemporary critics dismissed these efforts as hack work, a definition with which posterity has agreed, but most reviewers were forced to admit that even at her worst Mrs. Stowe wrote with fluid grace and captured the attention of her readers.

One novel of stature, *Old Town Folks,* was authorized for serialization in the *Atlantic* in 1868 and was published as a book in 1869. In it, Mrs. Stowe returned once more to her New England roots, and there are echoes of *The Minister's Wooing* and *The Pearl of Orr's Island* in the new work. The sweet, pure heroine, Tina, is similar in her character and religious fervor to other Stowe heroines, but Tina's beloved, Ellery Davenport, is at least somewhat out of the ordinary. Like Aaron Burr a grandson of Jonathan Edwards, he is a rakehell who hates more than he loves, and the reader who anticipates his eventual redemption is due for a surprise. Ellery gives himself up to dissipation, loses his mind, and meets his just end when he is killed in a duel. Tina falls handily into the arms of the stalwart Horace Holyoke, Mrs. Stowe thereby fudging a question she has raised. One wonders, as the righteous Horace does not, how a girl as upright as Tina could ever have cared for the licentious Ellery. Presumably she would have been repelled by him rather than drawn to him.

As fiction, *Old Town Folks* offered nothing new; virtually all of the characters had appeared in Mrs. Stowe's earlier books. It was lacking, too, in the impassioned strength that, despite its faults, had given life to *Uncle Tom's Cabin*. But the later work is undeniably a serious one and for certain reasons has even been regarded by modern students as her best novel. Certainly her picture of New England small-town life is realistic, completely authentic. To achieve this had been her goal from the outset. "It is my résumé of the whole spirit and body of New England," and no critic has been able to deny the accuracy of that observation.

Fields marveled that she could write the book when she so frequently interrupted her labors on it to turn out articles and other, lesser works. By this time she had mastered her craft, however, and was able to give each project the degree of attention she felt its importance warranted. She regarded her writing as a business, not an art, and nothing better exemplifies her professionalism than the sudden reversal of her position regarding the serialization of *Old Town Folks*. She had authorized its monthly publication in the *Atlantic* but changed her mind because, she told Fields, the book would enjoy a bigger sale without prepublication serialization. She proved she was right, for *Old Town Folks* enjoyed a larger sale than *The Minister's Wooing, Agnes of Sorrento,* and even *The Pearl of Orr's Island.*

The new work paid graceful, affectionate, and mature tribute to Lyman Beecher. He is reflected, in part, in many other ministers of her devising, but in *Old Town Folks* he lives. She performed the difficult feat of showing him objectively rather than through the eyes of a loving daughter. Like all Calvinists, and like his prototype, Beecher, the minister in this book was willing to admit that, hypothetically, man was capable of being a complete sinner, but in his ministry he refused to take that position, insisting that the corrupt and depraved behaved as they did only because of their ignorance of the truth. Similarly, no man would reject God after being shown the light; atheists simply knew no better and would turn to God when they became aware of Him. Certainly Mrs. Stowe was thinking of Lyman Beecher when she wrote that he worked incessantly with unflagging enthusiasm "in favor of some original-minded sheep who can't be gotten into the sheepfold without some alteration in the paling. In these cases I have generally noticed that he will loosen a rail or tear off a picket, and let the sheep in, it being his impression, after all, that the sheep are worth more than the sheep-fold."

The health and well-being of Frederick, however, took precedence over Mrs. Stowe's other concerns, and immediately after the close of the Civil War, in 1865, when his condition showed no improvement, she began to seek a new vocation for him, one that would keep him out-of-doors. A number of possible projects came to mind, and one seemed perfect for her purposes. She would rent an old cotton plantation called Laurel Grove on the west bank of the St. Johns River in Florida, not far from the village of Orange Park. There she would install Fred as manager (although he knew literally nothing about growing and marketing cotton). He would work in the open all year, his health would be restored, and not only would she make a profit from the enterprise, but she and Professor Stowe would go to Florida themselves each winter to escape from the New England cold they increasingly disliked.

The plantation was rented early in 1866, more than one hundred former slaves were hired, and Fred took charge. Professor and Mrs. Stowe joined him for the winter of 1866-67, displaying astonishing courage or, perhaps, foolhardiness. Florida, unflinchingly loyal to the Confederacy throughout the war, was in chaos, as was the rest of the South. Thousands of blacks had not yet found work, the former economy of the state had broken down, and opportunists from the North, known as carpetbaggers, were drifting in, looking for ways to earn a quick fortune. Confederate veterans, their fathers, and their brothers felt compelled to form vigilante bands to protect what little was left of their property and fortunes.

President Lincoln was dead, assassinated by John Wilkes Booth, so no living person was more universally hated in the deep South than Harriet Beecher Stowe. Life was cheap, Federal troops were finding it difficult to maintain order, and Mrs. Stowe's friends urged her to reconsider her plans to travel to Florida.

She shrugged off their warnings: She and her husband were law-abiding Christians, and no one would be foolish enough to harm a retired theologian and his dowdy, middle-aged wife. The Stowes went off to Florida soon after Thanksgiving and enjoyed the winter. The defeated Southerners had not abandoned their courtesy or their good manners, and, although they did not actively seek the company of the woman who had done so much to bring the slavery issue to a head, Mrs. Stowe was not molested, threatened, or insulted. She worked serenely in a sunlit room, and the professor wrote outdoors, eventually completing his own manuscript.

But after having leased the plantation for two years, Mrs. Stowe was forced to admit the project was costing her too much and had to be abandoned. Fred was inept as a plantation manager, as well as alcoholic. The former slaves who worked for him took advantage of his lack of experience, doing as little work as they could, and what had been a profitable enterprise before the war was losing money every month.

Still Mrs. Stowe would not admit defeat, and in 1868 she bought land at nearby Mandarin, on the east bank of the St. Johns River. This property of two hundred acres produced an annual yield of seventy-five thousand oranges, she wrote the Reverend Charles Stowe, and she expected it to show a profit of two thousand dollars per year.

These hopes were not realized. Fred remained incapable of controlling his drinking, much less of managing a property, and had to be sent to an institution for several months. He returned to Mandarin after his release, and his parents, determined that he should succeed, again placed him in charge. He remained there until the early 1870s, desperately unhappy, his situation never improving, his mismanagement a constant drain on his parents, who now made it a habit to spend every winter at Mandarin.

One of Mrs. Stowe's business ventures paid off handsomely, to the surprise of her publishing associates, although she herself had anticipated no other result. Calvin Stowe's *Origin and History of the Books of the Bible* was a resounding success. Fields distributed it to booksellers for a token fee, expecting a loss, but even he made money. Scholars and reviewers were unanimous in their praise of a work frequently called monumental, and the world learned what Mrs. Stowe had long known, that her husband was a man of towering intellect with an encyclopedic knowledge of the Bible and its background. It was gratifying, too, that the book earned a profit of more than thirteen thousand dollars.

One of the most interesting postwar phenomena was the new attitude adopted toward Mrs. Stowe by the South. Unlike many in the North who believed the last ounce of retribution should be exacted from the defeated Confederacy, she took the position that compassion was both Christian and sensible. In article after article, she argued that failure on the part of the North to extend the hand of brotherhood to the South would be harmful to the entire nation. As fully as anyone in her time she grasped the significance of Abraham Lincoln's plea in his Second Inaugural Address: "With malice toward none; with charity for all; with firmness in the right, as God gives us to see the right, let us strive on to finish the work we are in." Quoting the speech frequently in her own writing, she had considerable influence in making it one of the most famous addresses in the history of the United States.

She believed, too, that it was a mistake to grant the franchise to the freed slaves too quickly, that the whole country, including the blacks themselves, would suffer if the responsibilities of citizenship were piled on their shoulders before they were ready to assume such burdens. Acting in accordance with her beliefs, she founded a school for former slaves at Mandarin through the auspices of the Episcopal church and not only was the major contributor to the institution but taught there herself every winter.

One of the many educators interested in her efforts was the South's foremost hero, and one of the greatest military leaders in history, Robert E. Lee. Soon after the end of the war, he became president of Washington College at Lexington, Virginia, which later became Washington and Lee University. He watched the progress of Mrs. Stowe's work, expressing his approval both in private and public. Lee's blessing alone was enough to win Mrs. Stowe the support of thousands in the South, but even the skeptics changed their attitude toward her when she remained constant in her advocacy of moderation and taught for year after year at Mandarin without seeking or accepting praise. In the 1870s, when she visited New Orleans and other major cities in the South, huge crowds gathered to cheer her. But the tribute she most appreciated was accorded her by her Mandarin neighbors. When tourists from the North appeared in the area, and wanted to see Mrs. Stowe's house, they made it their business to reply, "There are no strangers living here."

16

In 1869 the ghost of Lady Byron prompted Harriet Beecher Stowe to initiate the most publicly painful incident in her life. Precisely half a century earlier, in 1819, Lord Byron had taken as his last mistress Countess Teresa Guiccioli, then only twenty years old, and she had remained with him during the last years of his life. She had left her husband, an elderly eccentric nobleman, for Byron, who developed an interest in the cause of Italian republicanism through her father and brother, both revolutionary agitators. Countess Guiccioli became well acquainted with Mary and Percy Bysshe Shelley, Leigh Hunt, and other friends of Byron who later achieved great fame of their own, and was accepted by them.

The countess had a story to tell, and, as an old lady, late in 1868, she told it, publishing her memoirs in London. The book contained little that was new about Lord Byron and created only a small ripple of interest, but one of Mrs. Stowe's English friends sent her a copy. To her horror and indignation she discovered that the countess disparaged her late good friend Lady Byron.

Harriet Beecher Stowe needed no other encouragement. The time had come to set the record straight, to reveal the secret Lady Byron had told her, and to make it clear to the entire world that the great poet had been morally bankrupt.

Thomas Moore had already told the story of Byron's relations with his half sister in his biography of the poet, but Mrs. Stowe either had not seen the book or had shrugged it off. Some of Mrs. Stowe's early biographers wondered what had now unleashed her fury, but she made her feelings very clear in a letter she wrote before preparing her bombshell.

> The reading world of America has lately been presented with a book which is said to sell rapidly, and to meet with universal favor, in which the mistress of Lord Byron, the Countess Guiccioli, comes before the world to vindicate his fame from the slanders cast upon him by his wife. . . . A narrow-minded, cold-hearted precision, without intellect to comprehend his genius, or heart to feel for his temptations, formed with him one of those mere worldly marriages common in high life; and finding that she could not reduce him to the mathematical proprieties and conventional rules of her own mode of life, suddenly, and without warning, abandoned him in the most cruel and inexplicable manner. . . . This sudden abandonment drew upon him a storm of scandalous stories which his wife never contradicted. . . . The sensitive victim was driven from England and doomed to be a lonely wanderer on foreign shores. . . . In Italy, under bluer skies, and among a gentler people with more tolerant modes of judgment, he found peace and consolation. A lovely young countess, breaking her family ties for his sake, provides the blissful retirement and domestic life for which he was so fitted. . . . Under the elevating influence of love he rises at last to higher realms of moral excellence, becomes the savior of Greece and dies untimely, leaving a nation to mourn.

Friendship for Lady Byron cannot fully explain the intensity of Mrs. Stowe's scorn. The question remains why she reacted so violently to Teresa Guiccioli's book, why she was so stubbornly insistent on publishing her reply to it when she was advised by everyone whose opinion she respected that she would do herself great harm. Students of the period have indulged in speculation about Mrs. Stowe's possible motives for more than a century. Some have said she was more of a feminist than she knew, while a number have indicated that she felt a need to release the anger and frustration that had been building within her because of her inability to curb Frederick's alcoholism. Certainly these may have been contributing factors, but her basic reason we may guess fairly certainly at: Throughout her life, as her books, articles, and essays make clear, Mrs. Stowe, a few exceptions to the contrary, despised women like the countess. Such immoral creatures were depraved, she believed, and the influence of one such harlot, like a rotten apple in a barrel, could corrupt an entire society unless its moral guardians rooted them out. As her entire career so clearly demonstrated, Mrs. Stowe—like all the Beechers—regarded herself as such a guardian.

After writing her article, Mrs. Stowe sent a prepublication copy to Oliver Wendell Holmes, giving him the background of her friendship with Lady Byron and saying that the meeting at which she had learned Byron's secret "had almost the solemnity of a deathbed confession." After decrying the Guiccioli book as being "from first to last an unsparing attack on Lady Byron's memory by Lord Byron's mistress," she made her own position plain. "I want, *not* your advice as to whether the main facts shall be told, for on this point I am so resolved that I frankly say advice would do me no good. But you might help me, with your delicacy and insight, to make *the manner of telling* more perfect." Whether Holmes offered editorial assistance is not known, but he was consulted by the nervous staff of the *Atlantic* and urged them to publish the article, even though he predicted there would be "volcanic eruptions, with lava flowing everywhere."

Mrs. Stowe's entire family urged her to forget the piece. The professor said it would do no good and that she risked tarnishing her own name and reputation. Charles agreed with him. Mary Perkins remained adamantly opposed to the idea, as she had for years, and the Reverend Edward Beecher, the Reverend Charles Beecher, and the Reverend Henry Ward

Beecher echoed her objections. The author remained unmoved. She was defending Lady Byron against unjust and unprovoked attack, she said, and she had taken care not to assault Byron too heavily. In fact, she mentioned his affair with Augusta Leigh only lightly, almost in passing. No one, including Mr. and Mrs. Fields, could persuade her to change her mind.

"The True Story of Lady Byron's Life" first appeared in the August, 1869, edition of the *Atlantic,* which went on sale on July 21. It sold out overnight, as did second and third printings. The demand for copies remained so great that the following month *Macmillan's Magazine* reprinted the article, and it sold out quickly, too.

Even Mrs. Stowe was astonished by the violence of the reaction. Rarely, if ever, has a magazine article created such a storm, and the controversy lasted for the better part of a century. Her supporters were few, her detractors many and vocal, and what outraged Mrs. Stowe were the attacks on her veracity. She offered no proof of Byron's incest but had relied on her memory of what Lady Byron allegedly had said to her. Preposterous though it seemed to her, people were actually accusing Harriet Beecher Stowe of telling a deliberate untruth, creating a sensation for its own sake.

Friends like Holmes, who wrote her a strong letter of support, rallied to Mrs. Stowe's cause, but they were badly outnumbered. The newspapers of the United States and Great Britain were filled for months with letters disparaging her, editorials censuring her, and cartoons ridiculing her. She was called a hack writer jealous of Byron's greater renown, a meddler, a frustrated moralist who would be better off minding her own business.

"Mrs. Stowe has done irreparable harm to the very calling which supports her," the *New York Post* declared. The *London Daily Telegraph* was even more severe, saying she had to bear "the stigma of having revealed a dead secret without cause, without authority, and without confirmatory proof."

A member of the United States House of Representatives offered an apology to Great Britain, calling Mrs. Stowe "a mere sensationalist writer," and adding insult to injury with

"Nothing from her pen is considered reliable by the American public." A member of the House of Commons went even farther and proposed that Mrs. Stowe be barred for life from paying another visit to the British Isles so she could indulge in no more mischief-making.

American magazines had the time of their lives, and only the sedate *Godey's* ignored the controversy. *Harper's,* with mock seriousness, outlined a complicated "morality test" to which all the great figures of literature should be subjected before their works could be sold in the United States or taught in American schools. *Gentlemen's Magazine* published an article called "The True Story of Mrs. Shakespeare's Life," written by "a descendant of Harriet B. Cherstow."

A number of Mrs. Stowe's more incensed critics wrote entire books in rebuttal. *The Stowe-Byron Controversy,* a supposedly factual account that was actually heavily slanted in Lord Byron's favor, was prepared by the editors of a popular London magazine, *Once a Week,* and became a best-seller in both Great Britain and America. It was rivaled in impact by *A Vindication of Lord Byron,* whose author, Alfred Austin, expressed his indignation in no uncertain terms.

> To the end of time Byron and his verses will be among the most cherished possessions of mankind; and if posterity deigns to preserve the memory of this foul fable in connection with his name, it will be only to remember that it was concocted by a woman of a very peculiar temperament and not gifted with a very fine sense of justice, first publicly narrated by an American writer of romances, published by a magazine somewhat in need of notoriety, accepted for the moment by the prurient and the incurable lovers of scandal, but after due scrutiny and just reflection entirely repudiated by the definitive voice of an offended people.

Dr. Holmes took the lead in defending the integrity of Mrs. Stowe and the word of Lady Byron, but his arguments were necessarily based on presumption rather than fact. He summarized his rebuttal in a long letter he wrote to Mrs. Stowe on September 25, 1869. An excerpt indicates how hard he had to labor.

> That Lady Byron believed and told you the story will not be questioned by any but fools and malignants. Whether her belief was well founded there may be positive evidence in existence to show affirmatively. The fact that her statement is not peremptorily contradicted by those most likely to be acquainted with the facts of the case is the one result so far which is forcing itself into unwilling recognition. I have seen nothing, in the various hypotheses brought forward, which did not to me involve a greater improbability than the presumption of guilt. Take that, for witness, that Byron accused himself, through a spirit of perverse vanity, of crimes he had not committed. How preposterous! He would stain the name of a sister, whom, on the supposition of his innocence, he loved with angelic ardor as well as purity, by associating it with such an infamous accusation.

What shocked Mrs. Stowe was the indifference of her critics to her strong stand in favor of Lady Byron. No one on either side of the Atlantic cared in the least about the purity of Lady Byron or the corruption of Teresa Guiccioli. Friend and foe alike paid no heed to the gallant efforts made by a Christian lady to salvage and rebuild her shattered life. The interest of every reader and every critic was centered on the question of Lord Byron's alleged incest. Mrs. Stowe was disgusted.

For a short time in the autumn of 1869, she was able to put the problem out of her mind because Georgiana gave birth to a son, her first grandchild. She wrote to Mrs. Fields, "I am... being first lady-in-waiting to his new majesty... getting to be an old fool of a grandma, and to think there is no bliss under heaven to compare with a baby."

The storm continued to rage, however, and it became impossible for her to ignore it. Her critics were still attacking her integrity, paying little or no attention to her defense of

Lady Byron and concentrating their fire on her lack of proof to substantiate her sensational charge against Lord Byron. No Beecher could turn the other cheek forever, and she decided she had to justify her position. Her family, Mrs. Fields, and many others urged her not to add fuel to the flames, saying the controversy would die away if she kept silent. But Mrs. Stowe insisted that was a coward's way out. Attempts were being made to stain her good name, and the situation had become intolerable.

She returned to her writing desk and put the whole story of her friendship with Lady Byron, including their entire correspondence, into a new book, *Lady Byron Vindicated,* which was published in 1870. Not satisfied with this endeavor, she prepared a revised and enlarged version for her English public, calling it *The History of the Byron Controversy.* It was published in London late in 1870.

Neither of these volumes contained new information or added data of any significance to her side of the argument. Her story still depended solely on the truth of what Lady Byron had told her, but her insistence that her friend was an honorable woman who could not have lied about so important a matter failed to convince her critics.

Had Mrs. Stowe maintained at least some measure of objectivity she might have emerged from the fight with her dignity and stature relatively intact. But, in her fury, she ventured the opinion that her foes were defending Lord Byron because he was a fellow male, and that her word and Lady Byron's were being doubted because they were women. The world was not prepared to accept a feminist argument in 1870, and her critics laughed at her. She compounded her problem by attacking Byron's poetry, abandoning both her literary judgment and her common sense when she referred repeatedly to his "filthy, ghastly writings." This assault made her doubly vulnerable, but she was so incensed she became incapable of separating Byron's dissolute private life from his work.

Good friends like Dr. Holmes realized she had lost the battle but were afraid to say too much, either in person or in their correspondence with her. George Eliot went farther than most in a letter to Mrs. Stowe written on December 10, 1869, in which she said:

> In the midst of your trouble I was often thinking of you, for I feared that you were undergoing a considerable trial from the harsh and unfair judgments, partly the fruit of hostility glad to find an opportunity for venting itself, and partly of that unthinking cruelty which belongs to hasty anonymous journalism. For my own part, I should have preferred that the Byron question should never have been brought before the public, because I think the discussion of such subjects is injurious socially. But with regard to yourself, dear friend, I feel sure that, in acting on a different basis of impressions, you were impelled by pure, generous feeling. Do not think that I would have written to you of this point to express a judgment. I am anxious only to convey to you a sense of my sympathy and confidence, such as a kiss and a pressure of the hand could give if I were near you.

Ultimately Mrs. Stowe appears to have realized that she made the worst mistake of her professional life when she publicized Lady Byron's confidences. Her son Charles was apologetic in the biography of his mother that he wrote late in her life, calling the matter one of her "most disagreeable experiences." She refused to back down in public, however, and insisted on preparing a statement of her own for inclusion in the biography. He dutifully published it, although she added nothing of consequence to what she had said in her original article and the two books that followed it. To the end of her days, she remained unswervingly loyal to her dear friend.

The long, angry dispute took its toll, however, and by 1871 Mrs. Stowe's fatigue was genuine. Sixty years old and world-renowned for almost two decades, she had written a vast body of work and wanted a sabbatical from her labors. Her exhaustion made her particularly vulnerable to yet another blow, from which she never completely recovered.

Frederick Stowe was still fighting his lonely battle against alcoholism, in Florida, and no improvement in his health was discernible. His parents, who had always been rejuvenated by the sea, suggested that he take a long voyage, and he agreed, going to San Francisco to take passage across the Pacific. There he disappeared without a trace. Efforts were made by the family, through the police and private investigators, to learn what had become of him. Various theories were advanced: He had committed suicide; he had been murdered; he had shipped out as a sailor under an assumed name, determined to terminate his parents' continuing heartache. No evidence of any kind could be found to substantiate any of these theories. Whatever may have happened to Frederick Stowe, no clues were ever found.

Professor and Mrs. Stowe were stricken, and the tragedy aged them overnight. Mrs. Stowe's gray hair turned white. She grieved in private for her lost son, never mentioning him in conversation, never expressing her feelings in correspondence with relatives or friends. After Henry's death, she had referred to her loss for many years, finding a natural outlet for her feelings in her letters. But she had suffered for years on Frederick's behalf, and the final blow was so great that she herself could survive only by burying it within her.

She would recover sufficiently to resume her career, and a number of new triumphs, some of them surprising, still awaited her. But the tragedy robbed her work of both spontaneity and emotional intensity, and although it continued to enjoy enormous sales, her best efforts were behind her. The disappearance of Frederick, Henry Ward Beecher believed, turned his sister in the direction of old age.

17

In the early 1870s, the pace of industrial encroachment on the Stowes' Hartford mansion increased. A new factory was built within sight, and the Park River, which flowed through the property, was renamed the Hog River. The cost of the mansion's upkeep remained exorbitant, and it was constantly in need of major repairs.

Mrs. Stowe hated to think of moving, but the family gave her no peace. The professor, who had never felt at home there, complained constantly. The twins added their increasingly influential voices to his. Eliza and Hattie, who never married, had taken charge of domestic operations by the 1870s, hiring and supervising the servants, doing the marketing, and keeping the accounts. They also acted as secretaries for their mother, scheduling her appointments, handling routine correspondence on her behalf, and, above all, shielding her from the outside world. She confessed to George Eliot that she needed longer periods of rest and could no longer work at her former frantic pace, and the twins saw to it that her tranquillity was undisturbed.

In 1873 they found a new house, on Forest Street, in Hartford and persuaded her to buy it. She sold the old place, losing money on the transaction, and was somewhat disturbed when it was transformed into a cheap hotel for transient workers. The new house, which delighted her, was also a mansion, but was so much smaller than its predecessor that she referred to it as a "charming cottage."

Through happenstance, a colleague a quarter-century her junior had moved into the house next door two years earlier. Samuel L. Clemens, whom the world would know best under his pseudonym of Mark Twain, would write much of his most distinguished work during the twenty years he spent in Hartford. Mrs. Stowe became acquainted with him and his semi-invalid wife, who shared her interest in religion, and they established a casual friendship that extended over the years. On occasion, they exchanged signed copies of their books, but there is no evidence to suggest that either of these giants of nineteenth-century American prose influenced the work or thinking of the other in any way. In due course, Mrs. Stowe also became acquainted with the members of Twain's literary circle, among them the writers William Dean Howells and Charles Dudley Warner, but they were members of another generation and regarded her with a respect mixed with awe.

Not even the controversy over Lord Byron diminished Mrs. Stowe's popularity with her reading public. In 1873 she published a new book, *Palmetto Leaves,* a collection of sketches and essays about Florida. Not only did it become an overnight best-seller, but, by the following year, real estate prices in the vicinity of Mandarin had doubled. Florida newspapers gave her full credit for popularizing the state as a winter haven for Northerners, and they did not exaggerate. By the middle of the decade, the railroads were offering expanded services to Florida from northern cities between November and April.

The success of Twain's *Adventures of Tom Sawyer* in 1876 pleased Mrs. Stowe, and she sent him a letter of congratulations from Florida, telling him with tongue in cheek that Hartford had become the "literary capital of America." In the main, however, she enjoyed few such pleasant moments in the 1870s.

Catherine Beecher, now in her seventies, suffered financial reverses and was forced to return, for a time, as headmistress of the girls' school in Hartford that she had founded. Thomas Perkins, Mrs. Stowe's brother-in-law, who was the one member of the family able to give her sound financial advice, died in 1872. Isabella Hooker was becoming increasingly eccentric; indeed, the family believed she had lost her wits. Although she had long been associated with Susan B. Anthony and other woman-suffrage leaders, she shocked Hartford society by going to Washington and delivering a long speech before a committee of the United States Senate in which she demanded that women be given the vote. Mrs. Stowe upheld the right of any Beecher to fight for a just cause but was dismayed when Isabella quarreled without reason with everyone in the family.

The most staggering blow was the scandal involving her brother Henry Ward Beecher, which broke in 1874. Prior to that time, however, Mrs. Stowe had forced herself to become active again, and set a pace that few people half her age could match.

Before Frederick's disappearance in 1871, she wrote a serial, *My Wife and I*, also published in book form in 1871. *Women in Sacred History*, a collection of nineteen pieces about heroines from the Bible, was published in 1873. Two children's books, *Little Pussy Willow* (1870) and *Betty's Bright Idea* (1876), both belong to this general period. She wrote articles and stories, too, for a half-dozen magazines, but principally for the *Atlantic*, and contributed several essays to *Revolution*, a monthly publication devoted to the cause of women's rights.

She helped Catherine Beecher in a time of trouble by collaborating with her and lending her own name to two books, both published in 1873, *The New Housekeeper's Manual* and *Principles of Domestic Science as Applied to the Duties and Pleasures of the Home*.

Pink and White Tyranny, published first as a serial in 1870 and as a book in 1871, was a venture into a new field. Her protagonist was a man, a metropolitan journalist, and Mrs. Stowe dealt at length with the complexities of city living, wherever possible including propaganda in favor of women's rights. *My Wife and I,* which followed shortly thereafter, was something of a sequel to *Pink and White Tyranny,* but was far superior to it. A third story in what has sometimes been called a trilogy, *We and Our Neighbors,* appeared first as a serial and then as a book in 1875. It sank to the level of the first, and all three books must be regarded as ordinary in all but their theme. In spite of her sorrows, Mrs. Stowe was still opening new literary frontiers: Through this trilogy, she became the first American author to deal with what subsequently became one of the most popular of subjects, the difficulties of living, working, and developing meaningful relations with other people in a large city.

In spite of her heavy writing schedule, which stunned her business associates, Mrs. Stowe felt she had too much time on her hands in which to brood about Frederick. Consequently, in the early autumn of 1872, she allowed herself to be persuaded by a Boston lecture bureau to make a tour of New England, reading from her own works. She began her travels on September 19 and brought the tour to a close on December 1, when she and her husband went off to Florida for the winter. During this period, she returned to Hartford for weekends when she could, and each day she traveled by train to another city.

What a change had taken place in this woman of sixty-one since she made her first trip to England and Scotland almost two decades earlier! On that journey it had been too painful for her, in spite of the recent success of *Uncle Tom's Cabin,* to sit on the platform during one of her husband's lectures on slavery or the evils of liquor. Now, without a qualm, she embarked on a new career.

Her letters to the professor during the tour indicate her rapid progress in courage. For a few days, she found her appearances painful, but she developed the critical ability to judge her own performance as well as her effect on her audiences. Somewhat to her surprise, every lecture was sold out, and, regardless of whether she read well or stumbled over her words, her public greeted her with volleys of enthusiastic applause. Best of all, she found she was making large sums of money. She hated the constant grind of travel, the need to socialize with adoring hostesses in every town. But the work, she confided in letters to her husband, was easy—well, not really easy but far easier than writing.

The unqualified success of the first tour impelled her to agree to a second, which was even more ambitious, the following year. She went to Chicago, Pittsburgh, Columbus, Dayton, Zanesville, and Cincinnati (her only return to the city where she had lived so many years; her nephew George Beecher dutifully drove her to see the buildings of the Lane Seminary as well as the house where she and her family had lived).

By her second tour, Mrs. Stowe was a veteran who had learned the tricks of the trade. She could make audiences laugh or cry at will and understood why her father, husband, and brothers so thoroughly enjoyed public speaking. Everywhere but Cincinnati, where she stayed with relatives, she insisted that the lecture bureau reserve her a hotel room so she would not be beholden to well-meaning hostesses who insisted on arranging supper parties in her honor. She could easily afford suites but said she needed only a small single room, and was secretly delighted when hotel managements occasionally gave her a parlor at no extra charge.

Mrs. Stowe was tired of the lecture circuit after her second tour and rejected subsequent offers from several bureaus to send her on the road again. Thereafter, she made infrequent appearances on the podium, consenting to give readings only when the entire proceeds were given to one of her favorite charities. In any event, she had other things to think about by 1874.

The Henry Ward Beecher scandal first began to brew in the autumn of 1872, although it was given no credence at that time. One Theodore Tilton, a member of the Reverend

Beecher's Plymouth Church in Brooklyn and Beecher's one-time associate on the *Independent,* claimed that the minister had engaged in an affair with his wife. He confided this belief to one of the most disreputable women of the era, Victoria Woodhull, an adventuress who had been active for a time in the women's rights movement and had earned her living as a spiritualist, lecturer, and newspaper writer. A frank and insistent advocate of free love, she was regarded as an outcast by most respectable people. This group did not include the increasingly eccentric Isabella Beecher Hooker, who said she was "proud" to call "the glorious Woodhull my friend."

Apparently, Victoria Woodhull first wrote the story of the affair in the summer of 1872, but no newspaper or magazine of repute would publish it. Henry Ward Beecher was the symbol of Protestantism in America, the most popular clergyman of the age, a leader in a half-dozen reform movements. As many as twenty-five hundred people crowded into Plymouth Church at his two regular Sunday services to hear his sermons, and he frequently had to schedule a third service. He was in demand throughout the United States and Great Britain as a speaker and received higher fees than any other lecturer of the period. He wrote regularly for a number of magazines, and it was said that he was far more popular than President Ulysses S. Grant.

He and his wife had ten children, and no hint of scandal had ever touched his name. Urbane and prosperous, he owned a summer estate in Westchester County, New York, overlooking the Hudson River, where he entertained some of the most prominent people of the period, among them his sister Harriet Beecher Stowe. The very idea that he would commit adultery was, as Mrs. Stowe would write, "an affront to Christianity itself."

Victoria Woodhull first made public her charge against the Reverend Henry Ward Beecher in a speech she delivered before a sparse audience in Boston in September, 1872. Newspapers ignored the allegation, and so she printed it herself in her own magazine, *Woodhull and Claflin's,* in an issue that appeared in November of the same year.

The magazine sold out, but Henry Ward Beecher ignored the story, and his congregation, almost fanatically loyal, stood completely behind him. For a year, Theodore Tilton did nothing, but in December, 1873, he suddenly was inspired to bring suit in civil court. Beecher informed his sister, then in Florida, but seemed unperturbed.

In January, 1874, the world press learned of the suit and created a sensation that was the wonder of the age. All at once, Beecher was forced to take the matter seriously and had to contend with more than the civil suit. A synod of the Presbyterian church appointed what was, in effect, an ecclesiastical court to determine whether his authorization to practice the ministry should be revoked.

The circus in both the ecclesiastical and civil courts dragged on for two years. There were so many twists, turns, and reversals in the trials that people at the time found it difficult to follow what was happening from one week to the next. Tilton endlessly withdrew and then renewed his charges. Elizabeth Tilton's virtue, or lack of it, was argued by attorneys on both sides, and the lady vacillated with maddening charm, one day denying she had been seduced, insisting on another that Beecher had been her lover, then claiming that he had tried to seduce her but had failed. Now and again, she added more spice to the proceedings by declaring that her memory had failed, that she could remember nothing of what might have transpired.

Victoria Woodhull returned to England, her home, and tried to recapture a few shreds of respectability by denying that she had played any role whatever in the controversy.

The Beecher family closed ranks, with the exception of Isabella Hooker, who insisted that her brother was guilty. She conceived the idea of denouncing him before his entire congregation in the early autumn of 1874, and Mrs. Stowe came to her brother's rescue. Isabella was afraid of Harriet, so for four Sundays Mrs. Stowe sat in a front pew, ready to stare her sister into submission if she dared to step forward. These tactics were successful, and Mrs. Hooker returned to Hartford in defeat. Thereafter, the only member of the family who would speak to her was Catherine Beecher, who said she was too old to take sides in family feuds.

The ecclesiastical court ruled in the Reverend Henry Ward Beecher's favor, but its findings were nullified by a technicality. He had to be tried a second time, and a second time the court ruled in his favor.

The members of his congregation refused to let him spend a penny of his own money in his defense and contributed to a fund for the purpose. Captains of industry, United States senators, fellow clergymen, and numerous friends gave freely.

An overwhelming majority of people agreed with Mark Twain, who expressed his regret that "so insignificant a matter as the chastity or unchastity of an Elizabeth Tilton could clip the locks of this Samson and make him as other men, in the estimation of a nation of Lilliputians creeping and climbing about his shoe-soles."

The civil suit, impeded by frequent adjournments, dragged on until 1876. Tilton's principal attorney, convinced of Beecher's guilt at the beginning of the trial, resigned from the case in its last days because he became certain his client was a liar. The jury could not agree, nine members voting in Beecher's favor, three condemning him. Tilton lost the case, and most people regarded Beecher as vindicated. A great public dinner was held in his honor, and the judge who had presided over the trial acted as toastmaster. Scores of renowned men stood, one by one, to proclaim their complete faith in Henry Ward Beecher.

That should have been the end of the matter, but students of the period have kept the controversy alive for the past century. Henry Ward Beecher himself was steadfast in his declarations of his innocence, but he did admit he had been indiscreet. His ministerial manner was benign, and he sometimes flattered ladies; it was possible that Mrs. Tilton read more into his attentions than he intended.

For two years, Mrs. Stowe made the defense of her brother her first order of business, when necessary sacrificing everything else for his cause. She was the rock on which he leaned, as did his wife and children. Anyone who knew Harriet

Harriet Beecher Stowe

Beecher Stowe expected no less. It is surprising that she maintained a remarkable objectivity throughout, although the drain on her emotions was great. For a long time, Henry Ward's unbroken success had made her uneasy, and on more than one recorded occasion she had chided him, warning him not to "let the fuss go to your head." Several years before the Tilton controversy began, she wrote to her friend John T. Howard:

> I feel, the more I think of it, that the world that hates Christ is just as real in our times as it was in His....I have pondered that question in relation to Henry's popularity; but I feel that the world really does *hate* him to a degree that makes it safe to hope that he is about right. Such demonstrations as now and then occur show that they are only waiting for him to be down to spring on him... in proportion as he makes Christianity aggressive on sin they are malignant and will spring joyfully on him when the time comes.

In May, 1875, when the storm was at its worst, Mrs. Stowe wrote to her son Charles, who was studying for an advanced degree in theology at a German university:

> Your uncle has had a degree of wordly success, he has had power and wealth and wordly strength, so that a rabble were following him for loaves and fishes using his name to sell quack medicines and him as a speculation. The Lord has lopped away all this worldly growth—none cling to him now but the really good. As to him he was in danger of over self confidence and of wandering into a sort of naturalistic philosophy. The trial has *driven* him to the Bible and Christ as a child clings to its mother. Best of all, I *do* believe that this severe affliction which has been to him a crucifixion has so entirely subdued his will to God's that he is now in that blessed state of rest which comes from having given up self altogether.

It was in her correspondence with George Eliot that Mrs. Stowe candidly and completely revealed her own state of mind and feelings in the crisis. In one of her longest letters, written from Mandarin on March 18, 1876, she unburdened herself as she had done in none of her previous correspondence with anyone. She recalled her childhood relationship with Henry Ward, explaining that she had taught him drawing and helped him with his Latin. She "saw him through college, and helped him through the difficult love affair that gave him his wife." She remembered the close friendship that had existed between her brother and Professor Stowe prior to her own marriage. And, with more than a touch of wistfulness, she said, "Ah! in those days we never dreamed that he, or I, or any of us, were to be known in the world."

Mrs. Stowe went on to summarize her brother's distinguished career, emphasizing the important role he had played in the campaign against slavery. Then she went on to list what she regarded as some of his other virtues.

> He has been a progressive in theology. He has been a student of Huxley, of Spencer, of Darwin,—enough to alarm the old school,—and yet remained so ardent a supernaturalist as equally to repel the radical destructionists in religion.... Then he has been a reformer, an advocate of universal suffrage and woman's rights, yet not radical enough to please that reform party who stand where the Socialists of France do, and are for tearing up all creation generally. Lastly, he has had the misfortune of a popularity which is perfectly phenomenal. I cannot give you any idea of the love, worship, idolatry, with which he has been overwhelmed. He has something magnetic about him that makes everybody crave his society,—that makes men follow and worship him.

"My brother," she told Eliot, "is hopelessly generous and confiding. His inability to believe evil is something incredible, and so has come all this suffering." Outlining the two-year struggle that Henry Ward and Eunice Beecher had undergone, Mrs. Stowe stressed the conspiratorial nature of the plot against him. Gradually her own feelings emerged, and it became clear that she believed Beecher's enemies were evil, jealous men, determined to ruin him because he had become a symbol of all that was good, of reform and charity.

> Never have I known a nature of such strength, and such almost childlike innocence. He is of a nature so sweet and perfect that, though I have seen him thunderously indignant at moments, I never saw him fretful or irritable,—a man who continuously, in every little act of life, is thinking of others.... In all this long history there has been no circumstance of his relation to any woman that has not been worthy of himself,—pure, delicate and proper; and I know all sides of it, and certainly should not say this if there were even a misgiving.

Throughout his long trials, Mrs. Stowe wrote, her brother never neglected his daily work, continuing to serve his congregation with spirited fidelity. In fact, he cautioned his parishioners not to become involved in his problems, which he refused to discuss, often to his detriment, with any but a handful of close advisers. Her loyalty was complete, her belief in her brother's innocence absolute. She never wavered in her support, and if she suffered any doubts regarding the final outcome of the trials, she kept them to herself.

Mrs. Stowe's strength during these years is all the more impressive because she continued to struggle with her own problems, and there was no one on whom she could lean for comfort or support. Her husband's physical condition was deteriorating rapidly; he retired immediately after supper every night, slept late in the morning, and showed little interest in anything but food when awake.

In the years ahead she would depend more and more on her youngest child, Charles, who would marry a sensible young woman, become pastor of the Congregational church in Saco, Maine, and then move to the Windsor Avenue Congregational church in Hartford. There, in the final decade and a half of his mother's life, he would become her principal source of emotional support.

But in 1876 Harriet Beecher Stowe stood virtually alone. She was wealthy, famous—and lonely. Her relief was infinite when Henry Ward Beecher emerged triumphant from his difficulties, but she kept her feelings almost completely to herself, indicating to everyone that she had always been confident of the outcome.

Only in one respect did she fail. Her new Hartford house was located only two blocks from the home of her half sister, Isabella Hooker, but, for the rest of her life, she refused to speak to Mrs. Hooker and cut her dead when they met by accident on the street.

18

By the late 1870s, most of Harriet Beecher Stowe's lifework had been completed. Finances were no longer a burden. Eliza and Hattie, far more efficient than their parents, held expenses to a minimum while still enabling the family to live comfortably. Georgie required no help, and Charles was already supporting himself, having been hired by the Congregational church in Saco as soon as he returned home with his divinity degree.

The annual journey to Florida was becoming too difficult for Professor Stowe, and he and his wife remained in Hartford during the winter. The twins, always ready to eliminate unnecessary expenses, persuaded their mother to sell Mandarin, which she did. The wrench was great, principally because Mrs. Stowe had maintained the fiction that she was keeping the place as a home for Frederick when he returned from his travels.

Most of the time she was willing to admit to family and friends that he had vanished for all time, but she could not completely abandon hope that he would reappear. Midmorning mail delivery time was the most difficult for her.

Eliza or Hattie would bring her mail to her study, after first looking through it. Mrs. Stowe would raise her head, asking a silent question, and would always be answered in the same way. This pantomime became a part of her regular routine, and persisted until the end of her life. She *knew* he would never return, yet kept alive a tiny spark of hope that he might write to her from the far ends of the earth, telling her he was well, that he had conquered his alcoholism, and soon would come home to see her.

Mrs. Stowe's many books continued to sell steadily, her annual royalties exceeding twenty thousand dollars per year, which was more than enough for the family's reduced needs. The demand for her work was still great, and Mrs. Fields, in an effort to shield her and help her conserve her strength, turned down most requests without referring them to her.

The success of her trilogy was reflected in fan mail and gave Mrs. Stowe a great source of pleasure. She was still able to be of service to people, she said, and she took delight in her ability to help them better understand their own problems. The evangelistic streak with which all the Beechers were endowed did not diminish when she reached her late sixties.

It was fitting that Mrs. Stowe's last novel, *Poganuc People,* written and published in 1878, should be autobiographical. Just as she had dealt with her husband's early life in Natick in *Old Town Folks* ten years earlier, followed by a collection of shorter fiction, *Old Town Fireside Stories,* in 1871, she now turned to her own Litchfield childhood in *Poganuc People.*

Her heroine, Dolly, was, like young Hattie Beecher, enjoying what she regarded as a normal, happy childhood. She was dominated by her older brothers and sisters, however, and in a family where excellence in achievement took precedence over all else, she was determined to accomplish more than her siblings and acquire lasting renown. Her father appears in the novel as Parson Cushing, whom Mrs. Stowe treated with love and a lively sense of humor. It is significant, however, that the parson was unable to comfort a parishioner whose wife had died, and that this task fell to Dolly, who succeeded by preaching the familiar theme that God is love.

Nowhere does her own emphatic feminism emerge more clearly than in her description of Dolly's reaction to a Fourth of July celebration. "She was a girl—there was no help for that; but for this one day she envied the boys—the happy boys who might some day grow up and fight for their country, and do something glorious like General Washington."

Mrs. Stowe remained constant in her other attitudes. In this, her last novel, a great revival meeting of religious converts is a highlight, and the owner of a tavern not only becomes reconciled to God but, as a direct consequence, permanently closes his tavern. Inconsistency was not one of Mrs. Stowe's faults.

She was not one to evade reality, either. The children of her Calvinist minister character attend an Episcopalian church one Sunday morning, and she describes their reaction in terms of her own experience. "It was in truth a very sweet and beautiful service, and one calculated to make a thoughtful person regret that the Church of England had ever expelled the Puritan leaders from an inheritance of such lovely possibilities."

Poganuc People is of interest chiefly because of its autobiographical revelations and because it was an indication of Mrs. Stowe's continuing preoccupation with the New England she knew and loved. Seen purely as a work of fiction, it must be judged as the least successful of her major efforts. She was sixty-seven years old when she wrote it, she had suffered many tragedies and hardships in her eventful life, and she was very tired. In a sense, too, she was her own victim. Her characters were not new because she had created all of them years earlier and used them again and again, and her faithful readers recognized these people as the clichés they had become.

Poganuc People created less of a literary stir and sold less well than any of her earlier books. Times were changing rapidly, although Mrs. Stowe did not realize it, and the public was developing new interests The United States was transforming itself into one of the world's major industrial nations with speed and efficiency, the antagonism between North and South was subsiding as a new generation grew to adulthood, and millions of impoverished immigrants from Europe were pouring into the country, their cultures blending in the American melting pot.

Mrs. Stowe clung to what she knew, continued to uphold her lifelong beliefs, and had little interest in new values. Hartford was still one of the more conservative New England cities, suffering few of the dislocations that the immigration of Irish and Italians created in Boston and Providence. Life remained serene, and Harriet Beecher Stowe, to whom the whole city regularly paid homage, was still the center of her own universe. She would have been startled had she realized that the book-reading public in New York, Philadelphia, Chicago, and other great cities was beginning to regard her as quaintly old-fashioned.

However, Harriet Beecher Stowe's seventieth birthday, in 1881, was a national event, and she was duly saluted by colleagues and the press as well as a dwindling circle of friends. The *New York Times,* the *Chicago Tribune,* and other leading newspapers hailed her in editorials, and the schoolchildren of Hartford were given a holiday in her honor. Henry Ward Beecher devoted a Sunday sermon to her.

She was losing neither her sense of humor nor her perspective. "My birthday," she wrote to the Reverend Edward Beecher, "is not Independence Day or Thanksgiving. If one lives long enough one is cheered for the simple reason that one has survived."

She held open house every afternoon at four o'clock, and her guests, many of them members of her church, knew they would be served tea and biscuits. She unfailingly reminded them that she was following a custom she had learned in France many years earlier.

Mark Twain, her neighbor, who was rapidly approaching the crest of his own popularity, had little in common with Mrs. Stowe but nevertheless admired her. He made it a habit to drop in regularly, pretending to seek her advice and often reminding her that she held a place that was unique in American letters. Her eyesight remained unimpaired and she still read many books, but it is not known whether any of Mark Twain's works were among them. She made no mention of him or his efforts in the brief letters she now wrote to the friends who were still alive.

Mrs. Stowe was still a celebrity, to be sure, and prominent persons who came to Hartford in the 1870s and 1880s called on her, among them Henry Wadsworth Longfellow, Ralph Waldo Emerson, Edwin Booth, and General William T. Sherman. Anyone of note who came to see Mark Twain was certain to be taken next door to pay his respects to her. Twain, who was genuinely fond of the ailing, aging professor, gradually won Mrs. Stowe's favor by telling her puns and feeble jokes which he collected for the purpose. She came to enjoy his company because, unlike almost everyone else she knew, he refused to treat her with reverence.

On Mrs. Stowe's seventy-first birthday, in 1882, Mr. and Mrs. James Fields gave a garden party in her honor. Georgie wrote a poem for the occasion, as did Whittier and Dr. Holmes. William Lloyd Garrison came, and so did Frederick Douglass. A number of younger writers were there, including William Dean Howells and Frances Hodgson Burnett. The highlight of the party, attended by at least a score of relatives, was a speech that was delivered, of course, by the Reverend Henry Ward Beecher. Letters and telegrams from other friends were read, and at last Mrs. Stowe rose to say a few words. For a moment she was shy, as she had been before, but everyone smiled at her, and she gained the courage to make a very brief address.

The greatest event that had taken place in her lifetime, she declared, had been the abolition of slavery. In the winters she and her husband had spent in the South they had seen black men acquiring property, becoming educated, taking responsibilities. "An old negro friend in our neighborhood has got a new, nice, two-story house, and an orange grove, and a sugar mill. He has got a lot of money, besides. Mr. Stowe met him one day, and he said, 'I have got twenty head of cattle, four head of "hoss," forty head of hen, and I have got ten children, all *mine, every one mine.*' Well, now, that is a thing that a black man could not say once, and this man was sixty years old before he could say it."

"That is the sort of thing I see going on around me," she said in conclusion. "Let us never doubt. Everything that ought to happen is going to happen." Those few words, Mrs. Fields later said, better expressed her basic philosophy of life than anything she wrote.

Mrs. Stowe's final work, a little children's book called *A Dog's Mission*, was published in 1881. In it she drew on her own experience as a sister, mother, and grandmother and demonstrated a great and sympathetic understanding of children, particularly small boys. Mark Twain kept a copy in a prominent place on a shelf in his library.

In 1886 Professor Stowe fell seriously ill, and when it became evident there was no hope for his recovery his wife refused to leave his side. His mind sometimes drifted, but when he was lucid she read to him, alternating between a life of Christ and the Bible. His interest in the subject matter, she believed, made it possible for him to continue the fight. She was at his side when he fell into his final sleep. What he may have said to her in his last rational moments was not revealed to anyone; as had been her habit for so many years, she drew a curtain of privacy around their relationship. She wept for him in private, but shed no tears at his funeral, saying he would not have approved of such a loss of dignity.

Her own decline after her husband's death was rapid, although in 1887 Charles Stowe revived his mother's flagging interest in the world by writing her biography and enlisting her aid in the project. In several letters to the Reverend Edward Beecher, she seemed lively and cheerful while the book was in progress.

Eliza and Hattie continued to keep house for her with their customary efficiency, the Reverend Charles Stowe visited his mother every afternoon, and Dr. E. B. Hooker, Isabella's son, to whom Mrs. Stowe's coldness did not extend, called, as the Stowe's family physician, every morning. By 1890 Mrs. Stowe saw virtually no one else, except when the Reverend Henry Ward Beecher and other relatives came to Hartford for the express purpose of spending a few days with her.

She no longer went to church, and the press began to call her "the Hartford recluse." Late in 1890, Dr. Hooker felt compelled to issue a brief statement. His patient enjoyed good physical health, he said, but sometimes suffered the mental lapses popularly known as a "second childhood."

In 1893, when Mrs. Stowe was eighty-two years old, she was bedridden much of the time, and the household staff was augmented by two nurses, one of whom was always in attendance. During her lucid periods, the patient was always cheerful and cooperative and read the many books piled up beside her bed.

During the 1890s, her reputation fell into a more rapid decline. The slavery issue and the Civil War were then history, and many of the other reforms for which she had campaigned had been accepted. Rhetoric had gone out of fashion in nonfiction. The trend toward realism in fiction had accelerated, and Mrs. Stowe's contrived plots, melodramatic incidents, somewhat stilted, romantic dialogue, as well as her repetitive characters caused her to be increasingly regarded as hopelessly out-of-date. Her preoccupation with religion was considered boring, and there was apparently no longer any novelty in her depiction of early New England life.

Other factors were also at work that contributed to the low esteem in which Mrs. Stowe was held. Principal among them, paradoxically, was the continuing success of *Uncle Tom's Cabin* and the play based on it. Public familiarity with both was so great that they inevitably were frequently satirized.

Not until the period following World War II had enough time elapsed for critics to see Mrs. Stowe in true perspective, and in the past thirty years her reputation has risen again. As she herself wrote, "True values are never lost."

Harriet Beecher Stowe ended her life peacefully. In her last days, she knew she was dying but remained calm because, as she told one of her nurses, she had been waiting a long time to meet her Maker. She died in her sleep at the age of eighty-five on July 1, 1896, and was buried beside her husband at Andover, Massachusetts.

On the first anniversary of her death, her cook, a black woman, was seen by a newspaperman putting flowers on her grave, and he asked her permission to photograph her. She refused. "This," she said, "is strictly between Mrs. Stowe, me—and her other friends."

Selected Bibliography

ADAMS, JAMES T. *America's Tragedy*. New York: Charles Scribner's Sons, 1934.

ADAMS, JOHN R. *Harriet Beecher Stowe*. New York: Twayne, 1963.

BARROWS, JOHN H. *Henry Ward Beecher*. New York: Funk & Wagnalls, 1893.

BEECHER, LYMAN. *Autobiographical Correspondence*. Edited by Charles Beecher. New York: Harper & Bros., 1865.

BRADFORD, GAMALIEL. *Portraits of American Women*. Boston: Houghton Mifflin, 1919.

ERSKINE, JOHN. *Leading American Novelists*. New York: Henry Holt, 1910.

FIELDS, ANNIE A. *Life and Letters of Harriet Beecher Stowe*. Boston: Houghton Mifflin, 1897.

FOSTER, CHARLES H. *The Rungless Ladder: Harriet Beecher Stowe and New England Puritanism*. Durham, N.C.: Duke University Press, 1954.

FURNAS, J. C. *Goodbye to Uncle Tom*. New York: William Sloane, 1956.

GILBERTSON, CATHERINE. *Harriet Beecher Stowe*. New York: D. Appleton-Century, 1937.

HIBBEN, PAXTON. *Henry Ward Beecher*. New York: Readers Club, 1942.

JOHNSTON, JOHANNA. *Runaway to Heaven.* New York: Doubleday, 1963.

PATTEE, FRED L. *The Feminine Fifties.* New York: D. Appleton-Century, 1940.

ROURKE, CONSTANCE M. *Trumpet in Jubilee.* New York: Harcourt Brace Jovanovich, 1927, essay in VERNON PARRINGTON, *Main Currents in American Thought,* Vol. 2, pp. 371-78.

STOWE, CHARLES EDWARD. *Life of Harriet Beecher Stowe.* Boston: Houghton Mifflin, 1889.

STOWE, CHARLES EDWARD, and LYMAN BEECHER STOWE. *Harriet Beecher Stowe: The Story of Her Life.* Boston: Houghton Mifflin, 1911.

STOWE, HARRIET BEECHER. *Works.* 16 vols. Boston: Houghton Mifflin, 1916.

STOWE, LYMAN BEECHER. *Saints, Sinners and Beechers.* Indianapolis: Bobbs-Merrill, 1934.

VAN DOREN, CARL. *The American Novel.* New York: Macmillan, 1940.

WAGENKNECHT, EDWARD. *Cavalcade of the American Novel.* New York: Henry Holt, 1952.

WILSON, EDMUND. *Patriotic Gore: Studies in the Literature of the American Civil War.* New York: Oxford University Press, 1962.

WILSON, FORREST. *Crusader in Crinoline: The Life of Harriet Beecher Stowe.* Philadelphia: Lippincott, 1941.

Index

Index

Index

Index

Index

Index

Sumner, Charles, 79
Sunny Memories of Foreign Lands (H. B. Stowe), 82, 88, 102
Sutherland, Duchess of, 90, 109, 143
Sutherland, Duke of, 109, 143
Swift, Jonathan, 17
Sykes, Georgiana May, 61, 112 (*see also* May, Georgiana)

Taney, Roger B., 106
Tempest, The (Shakespeare), 155
Tennyson, Alfred, Lord, 158
Thackeray, William Makepeace, 90, 94, 133, 138
Theological Seminary (Andover, Mass.), 76
Ticknor and Fields, 144, 154
Tilton, Elizabeth, 196-98
Tilton, Theodore, 195, 197, 198
Times of London, 115, 158
Tolstoy, Leo, 72
Trevelyan, Charles, 90
Trollope, Anthony, 144
Trollope, Rose, 145
"True Story of Lady Byron's Life, The" (H. B. Stowe), 185
"True Story of Mrs. Shakespeare's Life, The" (H. B. Cherstow [pseudonym, anon.]), 186
Turner, Joseph, 113
Turner, Nat, 104
Twain, Mark (Samuel L. Clemens), 192, 198, 206-8
Tyler, Eliza, 27 (*see also* Stowe, Eliza Tyler)

"Uncle Sam's Emancipation" (H. B. Stowe), 104
"Uncle Tim" (H. B. Stowe), 31, 33-34
Uncle Tom's Cabin (H. B. Stowe),
33, 38, 49-50, 64, 67-75, 78, 89-90, 96, 98, 105-10, 114, 134, 136, 158-59, 165, 177, 209
Underground Railway, 36, 63

Van Buren, Martin, 37
Van Doren, Carl, 74
Vanderbilt, Cornelius, 1
Victoria, Queen of England, 1, 57, 106, 108-10
Vinci, Leonardo da, 118
Vindication of Lord Byron, A (Austin), 186
Voltaire, 17

Wagenknecht, Edward, 75
Warner, Charles Dudley, 192
Washington and Lee University, 181
Washington College, 181
We and Our Neighbors (H. B. Stowe), 194
Webster, Daniel, 62
Webster, Frances, 120
Weld, Theodore, 67
Western Female Institute (Cincinnati), 27
Western Monthly Magazine, 26, 30, 31, 45
"What God Hath Wrought" (H. B. Stowe), 153
Whittier, John Greenleaf, 72, 103, 130, 144, 153, 155, 207
Wilson, Edmund, 75
Wilson, Henry, 163
Women in Sacred History (H. B. Stowe), 193
Woodhull, Victoria, 196, 197
Woodhull and Claflin's, 96
Wordsworth, William, 138
Works (Johnson), 6